Y0-BZF-218

Coming Clean
Journey to Wholeness

TAMMIE RATLIFF

Copyright © by 2015 Tammie M. Ratliff
All rights reserved.

ISBN -13: 978-1511661157
ISBN-10: 1511661151

.

Published and distributed in the United States by Ratliff
Publishing

Cover Design: Ratliff Publishing
Cover Photo: DeVashi Woods
Interior Design: Ratliff Publishing
Editing Services provided by Ratliff Publishing

All rights reserved. No part of this book may be reproduced
by any mechanical, photographic, or electronic process, or
in the form of a phonographic recording; nor may it be
stored in a retrieval system, transmitted, or otherwise be
copied for public or private use - other than for "fair use" as
brief quotations embodied in articles and reviews, without
prior written permission of the publisher.

Scripture references taken from KJV, unless otherwise
noted

"In The Morning" by Paul Laurence Dunbar. Poem excerpt
is taken from PoemHunter.com

MY OFFERING

This book is my offering to those who are stuck in the disparity of low self-esteem, feelings of unworthiness, guilt, shame and rejection. It is a lifeline to the religious, those who are held captive by the rudiments of that which has passed away.

To you all, I announce – YOU ARE FREE. You don't have to live under the cloud of your past any longer. We are now living in the Acceptable Year of The Lord. As you read my story, I pray that you will accept it as an offering that will cause you to come out of bondage and be FREE indeed!

CONTENTS

ACKNOWLEDGMENTS

First, I want to Thank God. In His infinite wisdom of who I would become, He has orchestrated my path. I Thank You, God, for the many opportunities you sent into my life to get my attention. Your Grace and Your Mercy has, and continue to carry me through. Thank You Father. I know this is just the beginning, and I am looking forward to the rest of the journey.

A huge Thank You goes out to my mom, Mildred Gales, and the late Arthur Ratliff for continuing to have children against the advice of the Doctor. Had you stopped with Arthur Jr., Tammie Michelle Ratliff would not have been born. Thank you! Thank you! Thank you!

Thank you to my children, Christopher and Matrix. You guys have loved me unconditionally. Even when I made your lives tremendously uncomfortable – you both still maintained respect and honor for your mother. You, boys, have so much greatness locked up in you, and one day the world will know your names.

Thank you, Margaret, for making me laugh. In times of hardship, you have a way of bringing joy into the every situation. Thank you for showing me that, "It's not that serious." You are more of an inspiration than you know. Love you so much!

Thank you to my church families: Livingston Chapel Missionary Baptist Church, Ghio NC; Kings Gate Church, formerly known as Sierra Christian

Center, Rockingham NC.; New Life Fellowship Center, Charlotte NC.; Temple Church International, Charlotte NC.; WE Church, Durham and Raleigh NC Campuses; and last but not least, the new-found New Covenant Ministries of Charlotte – Great things are about to happen for us.

To Minister Michelle McCorkle, you are my friend for real. I love you for your giving and open heart. I am looking forward to walking with you as God opens great doors before you. Anointed does not begin to describe the totality of who you are. We will forever be in covenant, and where I go – you go – just like that!

To Apostle Edmund C. Brown, thank you for our late-night talks and laughter. You are such an anointed vessel. Thank you for the many opportunities to share with those entrusted to your care.

To Rosalyn and Pam. Ladies, you two have told me the truth about myself on more than one occasion, and for that I thank you! With a personality like mine, I need people who can look me in the eyes and tell me the truth, the whole truth, and nothing but the truth … in love. Keep being bold and brilliant! Love you both.

To Minister Willie Mae Neal, all I can say is "THANK YOU" for being a mother friend to me. Your love for and faith in God inspires me to draw closer to Him. Love you!

Thank you to: Prophet Wayne Whitley, Pastor Eddie McLean, Pastor Timothy Newton, Bishop Kevin Long, Apostle James Spence and every prophetic voice that has spoken into my life. Continue speaking His truth in Love, and bringing about great change in the lives of His people.

To all other friends and family – Thank You for whatever part you played in my development. No one gets to destiny alone.

Chapter 1

THE 970

Mmm! The smell of "Wonder Bread" baking was one of the delights of living in Detroit. We lived right across the highway from the huge bakery that produced the famous brand, and the aroma alone was enough to send your body into a diabetic coma.

My dad was working at Chrysler at the time, and life growing up at 970 Temple in Detroit Michigan was pretty good. We lived in a three-story housing project near downtown Detroit. Almost every Saturday we were doing something as a family - from going fishing to hanging out at Belle Isle all day. There were some Saturday's that my mom, dad, aunt and uncle would sit around and play cards while we (the children) would either be outside or playing down in the basement. On card days, I remember all of us walking to the store to get NowLaters and Penny Candy. Back then they had all types of flavors: spearmint; vanilla; chocolate; and o so many other good and juicy flavors. But Chico Sticks, BB Bats, and Mary Janes were my favorite. Yum yum!

At the time, I didn't realize just how good we had

it, but we definitely did. As a family of 8 (six children and my parents), I cannot remember one time being hungry, and/or going without anything. My dad was a very hard-working man. Although he drank, he was a good man who took pride in his family. He was very protective of his. He was not a big talker, but if you messed with his family, you'd see a side of him that you'd wished you'd never seen, especially when he got drunk – a man of few words but would not hesitate to shoot anyone who threatened the welfare of his family.

I often watched him in his busy-ness. He was constantly doing something. If he was not working on the car, he was sitting on the dock of the bay, fishing. That was his favorite thing to do. After he retired from Chrysler, we moved to the south. After settling in, he continued his favorite pastime of fishing, but he also took on the responsibility of a large garden and tending to livestock, (hogs, chickens, etc.).

My mom was a stay at home mom for the majority of our childhood, so we always had that homey kind of home. My dad didn't want her to work because I guess he knew the importance of mothers being home with their children. I don't think she mind because she could care for the house and her children the way she wanted to.

Momma was a black Martha Stewart, so-to-speak. I remember recipe books everywhere. She exposed us to a lot of different dishes that she saw in magazines and books. She was always ordering recipe cards from somewhere. Once they came in the mail we had to help her sort them out according to their category. Entrees with entrees, desserts with desserts, and so on and so forth. I think she was a part of a club or something because many of them came in the mail once a month. I will say that her recipes were here prized possession.

We never worried about having clothes either because my mother was also a master seamstress. She would make most of our clothes – even the suites my brothers wore to the Kingdom Hall. Sometimes I look at her photo albums, and I can see the love she had for her children by what we had on. She believed in dressing her babies.

Of course, as a young girl I still coveted what the other girls had. I think that was just a part of growing up, though. However, I've always wanted more. Even then I was equating my worth to things external.

In the 8th grade, I wrote a classmate a note asking her for her purse. Back then we held on to our notes, and somehow my mom found it. She tore my behind to pieces. "Don't you be out here begging people for their stuff. You act like you don't have anything!" Whew! I r-e-m-e-m-b-e-r that whooping. Good grief-o-mighty. I bet I never asked anybody else for anything while I was in school. Jesus! She lit my fire for real. Momma was big on 'not asking'.

If someone gave us a piece of candy, she would make sure we didn't ask for it. I now believe that this is one of the experiences that shaped my mentality as it relates to asking for what I wanted. It has always been a hard thing for me to ask for anything.

School was my favorite place to be. I remember being in the second grade and being enamored by one of my favorite teachers, Mrs. Hewitt. She would sit and read these wonderland stories to us. The stories would come alive, and she would draw us into them, as though we were characters in the books. Mrs. Hewitt was such a master at reading. Her words were so vibrant and full of life. I could literally taste the foods she described. She was truly a storyteller like none other.

Mrs. Hewitt was one of the first teachers to open my mind to the world. She had a presence that caused me to dream of "better." The jewelry she wore was so elegant, and she had this beautiful silky black hair with a hint of gray. She looked as if she had Native American in her blood. I would watch her thinking,

"I want to dress like that." It's amazing how the very essence of a person can make you want to stand taller and be better.

I can still smell that classroom today. The air was a mixture of coolness like ice, Elmer's glue, and magic marker. Ha! I know it sounds crazy, but that is the only way to describe it.

Then there was Miss Miles, my third-grade teacher, she was a tall brown-skinned lady with light brown hair. I loved her class even more than I did Mrs. Hewitt because she really honed in on my strength in reading. She saw how smart I was and took it upon herself to nurture me academically. It was in her class that I began to win numerous spelling bees, and various other awards.

I remember when we moved out of the city of Detroit into Inkster Michigan, which was on the outskirts of the city; Miss Miles would send me Judy Blume books in the mail, and would encourage me to "never stop reading."

Side Note: When people believe in you - they will invest in you.

My performance in school was well above average. It seemed that learning just came easy to me.

As a matter of fact, I made the honor roll throughout my entire elementary years. One of my teachers even wanted to put me up a grade, but for some reason it didn't happen. I remember the conversations about it, however, nothing ever came of it.

By the time I was in the third grade, I knew I wanted to be a teacher. Every year our family would take a trip to the south. Oh, how I hated the south. However, this particular year – I believe I was in the fourth-grade – I'd asked my teacher for some of our old worksheets to take with me. I would sit and commence to teach class to my make-believe students, and then turn around and grade their make-believe papers.

When we moved to Inkster Michigan, things were a bit different. I guess it felt that way because it was such an unfamiliar place. I did well, but it wasn't like being in Detroit – the teachers didn't seem to have the same passion as my previous teachers. However, I will say, the school in Inkster exposed us to the arts. In the fifth grade, I remember receiving great accolades for the recital of one of Paul Laurence Dunbar's poems, "In the Morning."

"Lias! Lias! Bless de Lawd
Don' you know de day's erbroad?

Ef you don't git up, you scamp,
Dey'll be trouble in dis here camp.
Tink I gwine to let you sleep
W'ile I meks yo' boa'd an' keep?
Dat's a putty howdy-do
Don' you hyeah me, 'Lias-you? ..."

Nothing encouraged me more than being able to stand in accomplishment, even at that age.

Another of my fondest memories was being in the fifth-grade Christmas program as a ballerina in the performance of the Nutcracker. It was so much fun. I was somewhat self-conscience because of my size, but all-in-all it was a wonderful experience.

Speaking of weight, I was very self-conscious in school because I was tall and big. I always felt as if I was the biggest person in the class, and I had a tendency to shy away because of it. My classmates didn't make it any easier on me with their picking and carrying on, but through the years I tried not to let it bother me as bad. I know now that I was not dealing with it as well as I thought because I learned to internalize everything, thereby making things worse.

One year Miss Miles took a few girls to her house for an outing. We made yarn kites and did other fun stuff that made me not want to leave. When it was time for her to bring us home, she stopped by an ice cream parlor and bought everyone ice cream. I ate mine so fast that it made me sick. By the time I got home, I was throwing up. I went into the house, and Miss Miles followed. She told my mom what happened and ... well, let's just say the outcome was not pleasant. She told me I was greedy, and that I would not be going anywhere else. Boy oh boy, I could get myself into some terrible messes.

I always felt that I didn't fit in because I excelled in everything I did, and many of my classmates picked on me, calling me the teacher's pet. Having long hair and dressing in cute dresses didn't help either. Many of the little girls would pull my hair and call me ugly.

As a child, my main objective was fitting in, and when that didn't happen, as I have come to understand, I would turn to food for comfort.

The emotional pain I felt from being different from other kids was manifesting into stealing. I would go into the cabinets at night and eat whatever I could find. Marshmallows, the caramel candy apple wrap, my mother's diet candy, you name it ... I would sneak and eat it. I didn't know why I was doing those things because we ate well. But as I got older, I realized that I was an emotional eater. I learned early to feed my feelings.

I also learned very early on that it was not a good idea to say certain things. One summer we were headed south for our annual family vacation, and I heard my mom say something that I didn't deem to be the truth. So, what did
I do? I spoke up and said, "Ma, I didn't know you told lies." (0_o Close your mouth). Yep! I said that to my mother. Before I knew it, she'd backhanded me dead in my mouth. The blow was so hard my teeth started to bleed. Well, that was the beginning of my silent days. I think I sucked my thumb and slept the rest of the ride to North Carolina. It was not her intention to ever hurt me, but she was also not having a mouthy little girl questioning her integrity.

I was a very outspoken child, but after that, fear set in. I became fearful of speaking up, even if it was for myself. So again, I fed my feelings rather than release them. Eating just felt really good to me. It made me feel like everything was alright, even though it wasn't. I just didn't want to ruffle any feathers or make people angry with me.

As I've played many of my childhood experiences over in my head, I have come to understand that children are shaped by their experiences. As we grow up, unless we have worked through many of our negative childhood encounters, disappointments, and pains, we tend to project those same things onto other people, many times unaware. Thus supporting the statement that says, "One can only do what one knows." It's not an excuse to continue exhibiting bad behavior; however, this is one of life's most foundational truths.

To that end, we must learn to forgive others for what they did not know, and release ourselves from what we didn't know – keeping in mind the words of Dr. Maya Angelou, "When you know better – you do better."

Chapter 2

HOPE-LESS

Armageddon. This word right here had so much power in my life. No one could have ever told me that I would see the age of eighteen. I'm so glad that *they* were wrong.

"Field service. Ugh!" I did not like those Saturday mornings when we went out into what is known as "Field service."

Growing up as Jehovah Witnesses this was one of the requirements of those who were baptized. It was our way of witnessing our beliefs to the community. We'd go from door-to-door presenting the Watch Tower and the Awake. These were magazines published by the organization that promoted the beliefs of Jehovah's Witnesses.

I often felt embarrassed because being a part of this religion set us apart from so many things. We didn't celebrate nor participate in holidays or birthdays, and as an adolescent, it reinforced my already insecure nature. There were many times that I would lie to my friends in school because I was ashamed of being a Jehovah's Witness.

Not celebrating Christmas was the worse. When we went back to school from Christmas break, I would notice all the clothes and nice things that the other kids got for Christmas, and I would feel really sad. I didn't understand why we couldn't celebrate Christmas like all the other kids, and come back to school showing off what we got for Christmas.

In the mid to late 70's I vaguely remember the prediction of Armageddon (the end of this world). Although I was very young, the messages made an imprint into my psyche that promoted hopeless-ness. "I mean why plan for a future that you would not see." This thought caused a major battle in my mind. On the one hand, I was smart as a whip, and on the other hand I felt it really didn't matter because the world would end before I even turned eighteen.

In submitting to this belief, I never made real efforts to dream beyond high school. Although I did want to become a teacher, I didn't have enough faith in the future to even pursue it. While everyone else was talking to guidance counselors, I was merely existing until the inevitable happened. Due to some of the graphic pictures that were depicted in much of the materials at the Kingdom Hall, I would spend many nights looking out of the window to see if the earth was on fire. In my mind, it was if I was just waiting for that great and dreadful day to come, *then,* we could live in paradise after it was over. Lord have mercy, there was so much fear in my life.

When I was in my mid-teens, I began studying to be baptized. This was the step you took to openly commit your life to Jehovah. During one of our assemblies, I was baptized (almost drowned), and had now dedicated my
life to the service of Jehovah. In hindsight, my commitment was not genuine. It was fueled by fear and hopelessness, and you can never truly commit to anything if you have not been converted or thoroughly convinced through and through.

Authentic commitment comes when we first have a true understanding of what we are committing to, not out of a fear of what may or may not happen. *Entering into commitment for the wrong reason(s) will ultimately lead to regret.* When your expectations are not fulfilled you will throw commitment out of the window at the first site of trouble.

As I've pondered my experience as a Jehovah's Witness, I can honestly say that the only thing that really stayed with me was the fear of "the end." I can't say that I remember a whole lot of the teachings, but I do know how I felt – and it was not good. When you don't have anything to look forward to – you will find yourself simply going through the motions of life. No goals, no real aspirations – merely existing, waiting on life to finish its course.

Hope – Less

Chapter 3

"… AND BABY MAKES TWO"

It's 1985. I'm now a senior in high school. Life is still feeling empty, but I's workin' now!

We'd always worked a summer job, but now I was working a real job. Instead of working only during the summer months while we were out of school, I was now working after school and on weekends at Wendy's.

"Now I can buy me some 'stuff', the stuff that I want." This was my school of thought with my new job.

Wendy's on Broad Avenue in Rockingham North Carolina was my first year-round job. My dad had bought me a car from my high school sweetheart's parents, and I was driving myself to school and working. It was a gold-colored Chevrolet Impala. I loved that car. I'm not sure if I loved it because of where we got it from, or because it gave me a sense of independence. Anyway, it served me well.

My older brother was working at the Burger King, across the street from Wendy's, and there were some nights we would ride home together before I got my car. But this one particular night, October 3rd 1985, I didn't have a ride. I'd been in somewhat of a flirtatious relationship with one of my co-workers at the time, but until that night, it was nothing really serious. He would sneak and call me, but momma would interrupt the call and make me get off the phone, so William and I never really established a "relationship." He was a few years older than me, and already out of high school. I took a liking to him because I always loved tall men. This particular night he offered to take me home, and of course I said, "Yes!" I knew in the back of my mind that he was not taking me straight home, but that was quite alright with me. Needless to say, we ended up having sex.

When I got home, my heart was pounding. I was so afraid that my parents knew that I'd been out having sex, so I went into the bathroom and stayed in there for a long time, in hopes that they wouldn't ask me any questions.

The next day I felt really nervous. Pregnancy was one of those things that my mom always tried to protect us from. We never hung out with our friends, neither did we do much spending the night, and if we did, we were watched really close. As the days went by I began to realize that I'd gotten myself pregnant. That one and *only* encounter had produced my greatest fear – I was about to give birth to a baby.

Months went by, and I never told a soul. I noticed how my mother looked at me at times, but I would not allow myself to say anything. However, she did ask me about it several times, and of course I denied it. I was tormented everyday with the fear of telling my parents I was pregnant. I wanted to so bad, but I was literally paralyzed with fear. The fear of disappointing them; the fear of being a young mother; the fear of what people would think; and the fear of actually being able to deliver a baby. How bad would it hurt? Would I be able to do this?

Somehow I knew in my heart that my mother already knew, but I was trying to avoid dealing with it by lying for as long as I could. I was so tired and sleepy all the time. I would go to school and sleep through most of my classes. How I graduated? Only God knows. As soon as I came home from school, I would fall asleep wherever I sat. One day I came home from school and sat down in the living room and fell right to sleep. I could sense some eyes on me, so I attempted to wake up. There, staring at me was my mom and dad. My mom asked me again,

"Tammie, are you sure you're not pregnant?" Yet again, I lied and said, "No, I'm just tired." But again, I know she already knew, and I believe she was trying to give me an opportunity to talk to her about it.

Eight months have gone by. It's time to tell them, but how? I could not see myself standing face-to-face with them. I just couldn't do it, so I wrote them a note and left for school. When I got home, it was on. "Who's the father?"

"Ummm, his name is William."

"Where is he?"

"He lives in Polkton." Polkton was a small city I remembered seeing when Allan and I had taken a trip to Charlotte for Wendy's. Allan was a very close friend of mine. He was a white guy that I worked with and went to school with. When I didn't have transportation, he would pick me up and drop me off for work in his grandmother's car. We were strictly high school friends who enjoyed each other's company. One night after work he said, "You wanna go see the pink elephant?"

"What pink elephant?"

"In the graveyard."

"Umm, not really." I didn't want any parts of a graveyard at night. But eventually he took me, and there it was – a statue of a pink elephant. It was dark, so I don't know if it was a headstone or what, but I do know it was mounted in the graveyard.

We were mischievous too. One night Allan and I went through the Winn Dixie parking lot after work and stole some flowers. We ended up giving them to our mothers for Mother's Day. He was such a daredevil, and I was right there with him.

Then there was the time when he taught me how to drive a stick shift. He was really brave, because I had no clue. I almost stripped the gears right out of his little beetle bug car.

When I got pregnant I think it hurt him. Not because of any possible love interest, but I think he knew that it would change my life forever.

After I had my baby, I finally told my parents the truth about my baby's father. They wanted him to know about his child, and I could no longer hide his identity, so I gave them his full name and whereabouts. He didn't live in Polkton. He lived right there in Rockingham. I guess I was trying to be a vague as possible in the beginning because William and I did not speak anymore. After I told him I was pregnant he said it wasn't his, and he disappeared. I was so ashamed. The only thing that really kept me going were the comforting words of my dad.

I was sitting in my room crying one night, and he came in and said, "You and that baby ain't goin' nowhere, Imma take care of y'all." He always made sure I was o.k.

Now, it was time to go before the Elders at the

Kingdom Hall. I was so afraid. I knew that it was a big possibility that I would be dis-fellowshipped, but I was hoping that would not have to happen.

As I sat there being questioned about the pregnancy, as well as the act of fornication, I could see the hurt on my parent's face. It was heartbreaking to know that I'd caused this kind of shame to come upon them.

The verdict was in, "We are going to have to dis-fellowship you." Their findings were that I was not remorseful for committing fornication, but more so that I got pregnant. So no one could associate with me. It was painful to have to continue to go to this place, and no one could as much as speak to me.

I distinctively remember people speaking to family members sitting right beside me, but did not speak to me. I would even see them in the grocery store from time to time, and they would turn and go the other way. I could not comprehend how people could be so cruel. Even though I didn't understand everything about their reasoning – again it came down to how they made me feel; and that was *worthless and rejected.*

I was a seventeen year old girl who made a bad choice and ended up getting pregnant as a result. Why was the scarlet letter placed upon me? So not only did

I have feelings of hopelessness, but now I am feeling like a castaway.

On June 25th, 1986 around 7:30 in the evening, my sweet little baby boy was born, and I already had a name for him.

One of our neighbors had a son whom I greatly admired. His care and concern for his mother was impeccable, and for that very reason I decided to name my baby after him. His mom could do for herself, but he made sure she was taken care of.

He had the essence of a true provider, just like my dad, and yeah, I may've had a tiny crush on him, but that was not the main reason I named my son after him. His name was Christopher – but they called him Chris, and now my baby shared the same name, Christopher Shaunte Ratliff.

Shaunte was the name of a little boy who would come over to our house a lot. He was about two or three, but he was sharp. He was so adorable. My first boyfriend, Derek, was his cousin, but his family kept him all the time, and I wanted my son named after him as well because he brought so much joy to everyone.

I'd gone to the thrift stores and bought Chris all kinds of little outfits; socks, onesies, shoes, you name it. Wow! I had a baby! He was a good baby too. I can't remember Chris ever being a crier. He slept all night, and enjoyed watching TV. I started him on cereal early because my mother told me that if I put a little oatmeal (Gerber) in his bottle, he would sleep through the night – and that's what I did! And I never had any problems out of him.

Allan came over to see Chris, and brought a gift. We'd graduated from high school a few weeks prior on June 6th, and he was preparing to leave for college. So after that day I didn't see him anymore. He had a love for cooking and wanted to be a chef. He was good at it too. For my mom and dad's anniversary that year I had him to bake them a cake, and it was delish.

Jerry was home from basic training that summer, so he came by too. He couldn't believe I'd had a baby. We met during my junior year in high school, at which time he declared his love for me and pursued hard after me until we were considered "a couple." The relationship didn't last that long (because of me), but he continued to chase me. It felt really good that someone would want me that much. We'd never had sex or anything, and there was no pressure for it either. He was just determined to have me in his life.

He took one look at Chris, as he was holding him, and said, "I'm going to be his daddy." He said, "Tammie, I will adopt him and put him on my military benefits and everything." But I wouldn't let him. For some reason, since William was not there, I wanted Chris to carry on the Ratliff name. But that still did not deter Jerry. He continued to care for us.

Chris was my heart. I loved that little boy so much. However, somewhere in the first year of his life I got a taste of freedom – and for a while – I enjoyed that so-called freedom to the fullest.

Chapter 4

BOTTOMS UP!

"Girl you crazy." Those were the words of my best friend Trina when I told her that I'd never been to a club.

After having Chris, I knew I needed to make more money, so I got a job at Perdue Farms. It was one of the more stable company's in the city at that time, and the pay wasn't too bad.

Being around alcohol was not new to me. I'd watched my dad and other family members get rather toasted at times, so with my new-found freedom drinking almost came naturally. My very first freedom drink was E & J.

Trina had introduced me to the club scene, and it was all about getting drunk. Since I was somewhat wet behind the ears as it relates to "the world," I would often over indulge. My mentality was, "Why drink if you are not going to get drunk." For me, there was nothing social about drinking. I would drink so much at times that I wouldn't know how I got home. Drinking and driving were my norm on the weekends. I just thank God I had family to take care of Chris while I was out exploring and acting the fool.

When I hit the club scene I could not believe that I was out partying. To be honest, as much as I partied – I still did not fit in. Trina and our little crew could contain themselves while drinking, but oh no, not I. I was always over the top. If you wanted a clown, just let me get some liquor in me, and I would give you a show. I think I did it to feel normal, though. Somewhere in my mind I did not want to be connected to the "nice girl syndrome." Growing up the way we did, I just wanted to be like everyone else. I know that sounds weird because I'd had a baby, but for some reason, people still treated me like I didn't belong "out there." I know now that it was because they could see something on my life that I couldn't see. In all of my error, I believe that they could see the hand of God on me – and I wasn't even saved.

Working at Perdue would expose me to so many new people, people who were very experienced in life, including a married man. This is one of those things that I am not proud of, but it happened. I was young, feeling myself, and needed the attention. I was a very hippie girl, and men seem to love that. I had no clue as to who I really was so my physical appearance became the totality of my identity.

I spent many days sneaking around with another

woman's husband. So much so that people began to find out. But I was so cocky – I didn't even care. Then one day he told me that we would have to chill out because his wife and her family were asking questions. Our outings began to diminish, and eventually the relationship came to an end. Unfortunately, the drinking got worse. I was now drinking through the week, even before I went to work.

"Wake up honey." My line supervisor, Ricky, said sternly as he tapped me on my shoulder. "Wake up and come go with me." I was totally inebriated. I'd spent the night at Trina's house because most mornings we would walk to work, and when I got up, I was feeling like I needed a little pick me up, so I took a few shots of Seagram's Gin straight from the bottle – on an empty stomach.

If you've had any type dealings with alcohol, you know that drinking on an empty stomach will make you drunk quicker because it absorbs directly into your blood stream. So there I was asleep in the cafeteria – drunk. I'd already thrown up my guts, but it did not stop the effects of alcohol. When Ricky finally got me to wake up, he took me to the sick room where I slept the rest of the day.

We were working twelve-hour days, and I slept

until the shift was over. Lord, I remember having the worst headache. Ricky stopped by to talk to me before he left. His words were very gentle, but firm. He spoke to me as if I was one of his daughters, and said, "You are a pretty girl with so much going for yourself, why are you doing this to yourself?" I had no answer for him. I knew that he knew about my extracurricular activities with the married man – because everyone was talking, but he never brought it up. He simply challenged me to be better. He reminded me a lot of my dad. The care and the concern he was showing were beginning to make me think about my behavior, but just a little.

Not long after that incident I was released by Perdue Farms. I'd been coming in late and underperforming, but I soon got a job working at Walmart.

During my three-month tenure at Walmart, I met this guy named Brian. He was a tall dark beautiful man who was originally from Georgia but worked construction throughout the Carolinas. They were in the process of building more stores in Rockingham, and he was a part of the construction crew that was doing the building.

We began spending quite a bit of time together, and he eventually moved in with me. Brian talked about marriage a lot, but as much as I wanted to be in the relationship, I wasn't feeling a life-long commitment with him. I did enjoy our time together, but I just couldn't see myself married to him for the rest of my life.

At that point, he'd not given me any reason not to want to marry him, but it was just a feeling I had. We both wanted more in life and were willing to do whatever it took, but again, I felt a strong hesitation to make that commitment.

Speaking of "more," there were days I would go on shopping sprees and write as many checks as I could to get "stuff." Shoes, purses, clothes, you name it. I wrote checks, whether the money was there or not. At first, I could catch them before they hit the bank, but they slowly began to catch up with me one by one.

About a month into our relationship something major happened. One night we'd all gone out to a club, and of course I had to get drunk. Trina and I were still hanging tight and having our fun. After the night was over, Brian requested that we go to the trailer where he and the construction crew were staying when they first arrived to Rockingham. I knew in my heart something was wrong because he didn't say a whole lot. When we got in, he called me to the back room, and before I knew it I was seeing stars. He'd punched me right in the face.

He continued to hit me around my head and face multiple times. I was a fighter and tried my best to fight back, but he was just too strong for me. One of the guys ran out to my car to get Trina to tell her to come help her friend because they thought he was going to kill me, but somewhere between the licks I was able to get away.

I ran to my car with Brian on my heels, jumped in and sped away. He was trying to block me from leaving, but I was determined that if I had to kill him to get away – I would. He hung on to my side mirror until I got up enough speed to lose him. Lord have mercy! My nerves were a wreck. I was driving so fast on the highway that I spun around in the middle of the road.

About a week later, Brian called asking to come back, but I told him that if he came near me I would call the police. Somehow I got all of his belongings to him, and that was the end of that. I never saw him again.

I'd never been beaten by a man. As a matter of fact, my dad had never even whooped me. When he attempted to – he couldn't. He would say, "Act like you are crying so ya momma will think I'm whooping you." So for me, even with low-self-esteem, I knew I could not live with a man who hit me. I was not going to do it. That was the first, and the last time a man would put his hands on me to harm me.

Chapter 5

THE LOVE OF MY LIFE

Chris was growing by leaps and bounds, and I was finally slowing things down a bit. Still drinking and getting drunk, but not as much.

I'd bought a little gold-colored Chevette, and Chris and me would jump in that car and ride. I would dress my baby up in his two-piece short sets, buckle him in and we were in the wind like two free birds. By this time, I was on AFDC and food stamps because, after Brian, I refused to go back near Wal-Mart, so my funds were very limited. Anthony was in my life now.

He was a senior in high school, and I was a single mother with her own apartment when we finally started seeing each other. I'd met Anthony while I was a senior in high school, and he was a junior. I fell really hard for this man, but he had a bit of a situation, which made it hard for us to really get together in school. He had a girlfriend at the time, and she was pregnant.

From what I understood, they'd been together for quite some time, so he and I being on couple status in school was not going to happen. But, as you will find out later, a piece of a man was fine with me. He would spend many nights with me and then get up and go to school. He drove this maroon colored regal with a red antenna light. I'm not sure what you call it, but everybody had them back in the day. His car so ragged out, you could hear him coming a mile away. Ooo, I loved it. Now this man right here – was the love of my life.

There was something about him that drove me crazy. When I'd hear his car coming down my street, I would run down the stairs and stand in the door until he came in. On days he didn't come by, I would go looking for him. I pretty much knew that there were only a couple of places he'd be. One was his baby mother's house, so I would ride by there. Once I saw his car there, I was satisfied. I knew the next stop would be my house.

Once I met Anthony, I didn't have a desire for anyone else. I wanted to be with him for the rest of my life. He was the one man whom I'd do anything for – at any given time. He knew I drank too much, and mentioned it quite often, but it did not deter me. However, we did drink beer together.

Anthony was a hard-working young man and an overall good person. When he was not at work, he was sitting at the park on the North Yard with the other guys or at Carolyn's house (his son's mother). Yeah, I kept track of him, because in my head – he was mine. Trina thought I'd lost my mind because he was all I ever talked about. My club life changed drastically when we got together because he was not a clubber. He liked to sit around the house and drink his beer, which was alright with me, as long as I could be with him.

I was a real hoot back then. I remember Trina and I going to Anthony's job wearing these long Cher-like wigs in the dead of summer. One was blonde, and the other one was black.

Anthony didn't like that too well, and he let me know it. I think I was a bit too much for him at times because I was adventurous, and he wasn't. I was wild and he was calm, but he loved me, and I sho nuff loved me some him. Our favorite song was "Happy" by Surface. "Only you can make me happy-ee." We'd lie in bed and listen to that song at almost the same time every night.

I'd found a peaceful place in my heart being with him. Being considered his girl was the best feeling in the world. Now him ... I would've married without hesitation.

Chapter 6

I'S MARRIED NAH

Jerry was discharged from the army, and in hot pursuit ... of me.

Anthony and I were still seeing each other, but life was changing. I was now working third shift at ADS, so we weren't spending as much time together. By me working at night, it was hard for me to function during the day, so I slept most of my day away. Anthony would come over on the weekends, but that was about it. I was still crazy in love with him and would see him as much as my tired body would allow.

Jerry found out about Anthony when he came back and was extremely upset. There were days when he would go over to my mom's house and just sit. It really made me mad because it was obvious I was in love with someone else. Eventually, Jerry and I got to a place where we could talk about my relationship with Anthony.

I would cry on his shoulder when I felt that things were rocky with me and Anthony, and he would listen. There was nothing that Jerry wouldn't do for me. But I just was not interested in him in that way. I wanted him in my life, but only as a friend.

One night Jerry came by and told me that Anthony was cheating on me. I didn't believe him because I knew he would do anything to keep me from him. After all they had gotten into several face-to-face non-physical altercations over me, and I felt like Jerry was just pulling one of his stunts.

"They are sitting down there in the graveyard."

"They who?" With my eyebrows raised.

"Anthony and Keisha."

"Take me to them." I needed to see this for myself. In my mind, Anthony would never do this to me. Sure enough, there they were. I could not believe it. They saw us but didn't budge. I told Jerry to take me home.

On the way home we stopped by the store. While I'm inside Anthony pulls up. He comes in. When I look at him, disappointment fills my heart. Then it turned into anger. That was the end of our relationship. In my heart, I didn't want to lose him, but I think knowing that I had someone (Jerry) who really cared for me in my corner – I was able to see it through. Anthony was mad too. He wanted to know why was I riding around with Jerry, his rival of all people.

Anthony moved out immediately, Jerry asked me to marry him, and two weeks later, on October 23, 1987, Jerry and I became husband and wife. He'd actually sent me a ring while he was in the army, but I don't know what happened to it, so he ended up getting me another set right before we married.

During our nuptials (at the courthouse) I cried like I'd lost my best friend. My mom and dad were there, as well as a few other people, but I was so sad. I knew in my heart I didn't want to marry Jerry. As good as he was to me, my heart was still with Anthony, but a broken soul will do whatever it has to in order to get some relief. I didn't know that then, though. I just felt that Jerry was the best choice for me. All I was feeling was this man's love for me, and the fact that in the midst of everything I'd done, he still wanted me.

I was still in and out of court about the "bad checks" I'd been writing when we first got married. Jerry assured me that he would be there with me through it all, even after having to go to jail for a week. The first year of our marriage was rough. I was on probation and paying restitution for the checks I'd written, he couldn't find a job, and my favorite person on the face of the earth was dying, my dad.

My dad had been my biggest supporter all my life, and now he was slipping away. He'd suffered from congestive heart failure, and it was now taking a major toll on his body. It was nothing to wake up in the middle of the night and medics were coming down our hallway. Sometimes it was a heart attack, and sometimes they caught it at the onset.

I remember many times sitting with tears in my eyes just at the thought of losing him. There is no relationship like a little girl and her dad. When a dad is attentive to his daughters, it sets the tone for what she expects from other men. That is why I believe with all my heart I could not stay with Brian, and allow him to beat on me. I'd

never seen my dad fight my mom, so to me, physical abuse was not a part of my life's equation - not at all.

Jerry and I had been married for about a month, and things were getting ugly. He'd lost his job, and I felt like I'd been on my own this long, and I didn't need him. We argued about it for quite some time until finally he left and went back home with his parents.

"That boy back yet?" My dad said.

"No. And I don't even care."

My dad was very aware of what was going on, but he didn't say a whole lot. He was a thinker – I know that's where I got it from, and I could tell by his demeanor and questioning that he wanted Jerry to come back. My family absolutely loved him. There were many times I felt that certain of them liked him better than they liked me. That made me resent him all the more.

During one of my head conversations, you know the ones we have with ourselves. My niece calls them private commentaries. I'd been thinking about how much I'd done and how loose I'd lived. The guilt of it all caused me to beat myself to the core.

I didn't feel that I could talk my feelings through with Jerry because I secretly resented him. He'd never been in any trouble, and people thought really highly of him. I often felt that they saw him as a savior for poor ole Tammie, and I hated the very thought of that. In my mind – everybody was against me because of my behavior.

"Am I really that bad of a person?"

This was a constant question in my mind. Later, I realized that a lot of what I was thinking came from my own feelings of guilt and shame.

Note to self: It shouldn't matter what people think of you. What matters most is what you think of yourself.

On May 9th, 1988, the day after Mother's Day, the man whom I admired, loved and cherished passed away. Momma and I had been at the hospital pretty much of the day, but it was time for my brothers and sisters to come home, and momma wanted to be there to make sure everyone had something to eat – so we left and went home. My grandma, my dad's mother, stayed at the hospital while we went home. "Y'all need to get back here, something is wrong with Dune."

We'd been gone for about an hour when my grandmother called. "Lord Jesus, he can't die." That's all I could think about it. When I was younger, I always had this goal of moving out and bringing him to live with me. As a little girl, I always wanted to take care of my daddy – and if he dies, I would not be able to do that.

"There is nothing else we can do." Dr. Flannery was a very good physician and had done all he could do. My dad had been under his care for many years, so to hear him speak those words was devastating and comforting at the same time. I didn't know anything about prayer, or even seeking God about my dad's health - so I accepted it. Life was literally leaving his body by the time we got there. I was in the room when he took his last breath. It was gut wrenching to watch, but I know my mom needed my strength.

"Well, he's gone." I remember my grandma saying in the midst of my mother's tears. He was gone.

For many nights after his death I couldn't sleep. I

thought I heard him coming up the stairs in my apartment, but it was just my not wanting to let him go. About a month or so later the dreams finally stopped, but my heart was still broken.

My sense of aloneness was at an all-time high. Jerry was there, but like I said I secretly resented him, and with that came a lack of trust. I know he thought I was crazy because I was so on and off with him. My daddy was gone, and I felt that I had no one else to who would genuinely fight for me.

Chapter 7

ROUND TWO

Two years have passed. Jerry and I are separated, and it's me and Chris again against the world.

I'd wanted this for a long time because the marriage was not working and I felt stuck. My new job at ADS was paying pretty good, and I knew I could make it.

ADS was a manufacturing plant that specialized in women's undergarments. Being a seamstress, I knew this job would be a breeze, and it was. This was the one job that I absolutely enjoyed getting up at 5 a.m. to prepare for. Although we received a base pay, we were on production. Meaning we had to produce a certain amount in order to receive incentive pay. I always went over and beyond.

Chris and I have settled into our trailer, and I am dating another married man. By this time, I'd figured out that I really did not want to be in a relationship with strings attached. I'd see you when I wanted to, and dating someone who was married worked perfectly. I knew where he was when he was not with me, plus I was beginning to enjoy my freedom. In my head, I knew it was not right, but the hole in my soul was crying out for healing. I didn't know that then, so just like with the food, I tried to medicate with sex, alcohol and just having a plain ole good time – no matter who it hurt.

Jerry was doing his thing, and honestly I thought I didn't care, but there was an incident at the National Guard army that proved I did.

As much as I was doing you'd think I would've let Jerry go in peace. Nope! We were both out partying one night at the National Guard Armory, and things got real ugly, real quick.

Now, I'm out on the dance floor sweating my hair loose, and I notice Jerry over in a corner getting real cozy with this young lady. "I know it is a club and all, but have a little respect for me, your wife."

Wow! Who was I to talk? I'd been seen multiple times out with my married man. Everybody at work knew about it as well, so who was I to even think I could lay claim to a husband that I'd been so disrespectful towards. But somewhere in my mind I felt justified.

I confronted him, and of course I was not sober, so you know the altercation did not go well. He never would fight me, so I didn't have to worry about that; however, I was rather violent towards him. I remember going into my purse and pulling out some snips. They were miniature scissors that we used at work to cut elastic. They were sort of heavy but fit right into the palm of my hand.

I commenced to trying to hurt Jerry with them (I think I stuck him in the leg), but I ended up splitting my dress all the way up the back. You can imagine me out there fighting with all of my goods showing. I didn't know it until later, but it was too late to be embarrassed.

After it was all said and done, I remember thinking how hurt I was at the mere appearance of Jerry being with someone else. I didn't know I cared that much. But it was still not enough to stop me from doing what I was doing. I was determined to be "Miss Independent."

At the time, I had a Honda Accord with the flip lights, and I thought I was the best thing since sliced bread. I loved to play my music loud when I was riding because it made me look "cool." My soul was definitely in need of attention.

Jerry and I remained separated for about ten months, and almost immediately after reconciling I became pregnant with my youngest son, Matrix. People often ask me where did we get that name, and I have to be honest, Jerry is the one who named him. He told me that Arnold Schwarzenegger's character in Commando was named Matrix. Some people thought he was named after the movie, "The Matrix," but that was not the case. Those movies were not made until years after my son was born.

He was a tiny baby. Six pounds - five and a half pounds. Matrix was very sickly when he was born, though. We thought a few times we'd lost him. He had a condition known as acid reflux, and there were many times his milk would come back up after his feedings and choke him. When he was exactly a week old he stopped breathing for about 8 minutes or so. My baby was purple. Can you imagine holding your baby as he's has turned purple from not breathing? My goodness! That was a terrible time for all of us.

By the time we were walking through the hospital doors with him, the little booger started breathing. We would later find out that there was some brain damage, not extensive, however, he did experience a few problems as he got older and started school.

While I was pregnant with Matrix, I decided that I didn't want to go to hell. I would sit and reflect on all of the wrong I'd done and fear would consume me. So much so, that I couldn't wait to go to a church. I sat right in my car at my job at ADS and prayed a prayer of repentance. I wasn't sure about what to say, but I let God know that I wanted to be a different person.

As the years would go by, I learned that God was drawing me. Little did I know that He was going to do some great things in my life. I had no idea that even that moment was divinely orchestrated by God Himself.

Chapter 8

WOMAN THOU ART LOOSED

Get Ready! Get Ready! Get Ready! Bishop Jakes is mounting the podium. The excitement meter has burst, and we were ready for God to do something awesome in that place.

It's 1999. Here we are sitting at "Woman Thou Art Loosed," for the very first time. Jerry and I were still having marital challenges, but we were trying to hang on. Things seemed to be at a standstill, but I'd gone to this conference with great expectation.

Jerry and Charles had become best friends. They both worked at Morrison Correctional Institution and shared the love for motorcycles. Because of them, Tracey and I become very good friends. She and I had a run in when we were in high school, and it caused a great deal of tension when we'd encounter each other. But we were both saved and loving Jesus now, so the riff was not even and issue.

Tracey had been saved for quite some time, and I really admired her strength in the Lord. She would call me and encourage me in the Word because she knew that I was a babe in Christ. I was still carrying the guilt of adultery, but she never brought my past up. Our conversations were never condemning, and she never made me feel less than.

I often say, when I'm referring to her, that she mentored me in the faith and didn't even know it. She is the reason that my hunger for God grew. I would hear her pray, and desire to be fluent in prayer like her. I would hear her teach the Word, and it would stir a desire in me to be just as versed. That's when I began digesting the Word as if it was my last supper. I mean, I would fall asleep reading my bible at times. Then wake up and start reading it some more. When you first get a taste of God's Word, it's hard to put it down. It draws you!

I was growing and learning more and more as the months went by, and the time had come for me to transition to another church. I kept feeling this pull to go to this big church on the hill, Sierra Christian Center. The only problem was – it was a predominantly white church.

It wasn't that I was not accustomed to being around caucasians, because at the Kingdom Hall we fellowshipped with various ethnic groups, so it was not that big of a deal. However, what was a big deal was the fact that I was attending my brother's church, where he was the associate minister. It was a small family oriented Baptist church in Ghio.

I enjoyed going there, but I had this emptiness inside that caused me to long for more. I remember saying to myself, "It's got to be more to it than this." I just could not wrap my mind around *just* going to church for the sake of going. What I didn't realize was that God was working again. Drawing me by His Spirit to come up a little higher. Don't get me wrong, everyone has a path, and if it is for you to remain in a place, then by all means do so. But for me, God was doing something else. He used those experiences at Livingstone Chapel to acclimate me to the church environment. Remember, we grew up Jehovah's Witnesses and were told that if we went into a church we were considered apostates. We were even told that they didn't use their bibles in church. So God had to slow walk me to where He wanted me to be.

"Tracey, I believe God is leading me to Sierra."

"Well, go then!"

"I don't know." I didn't know what to expect, and I think I was feeling a little intimidated by the very thought of attending a ministry of that magnitude.

"Tammie, you have to obey God."

"Yeah, you right. Imma go."

It took me about a month before I actually went, but when I got there – I knew – this was where I belonged. The Spirit of God was so sweet. The worship experience alone was enough to keep you.

After being there for maybe two weeks, one of the ladies prophesied and told me that I was sent there to teach them how to treat black people. Wow! I was in the right place. They really embraced me, and it was a good feeling.

Now, back to the conference. The theme of Woman Thou Art Loosed that year was "Wailing Women Win." I'd never been to such a massive event, with so many people. There were thousands of women in that place. Women from all over the world – they even had women prisoners streaming in. We could see them on the jumbotron. It was awesome! Juanita Bynum and Darlene Bishop preached that year. But the height of the experience came when Darlene Bishop began to lead us into travailing prayer.

Whew! This was truly another level for me. I wailed so hard I fell out. While I was on the floor, I heard Bishop Jakes say that the heavens were open to us and that when we get back home, things would not be the same. Boy, was he right!

It was the beginning of a deliverance that I didn't know I needed. It was the beginning of my process to wholeness.

Chapter 9

YOU'VE JUST BEGUN TO SCRATCH THE SURFACE

"Sister, you've just begun to scratch the surface." That was the Word of the Lord for me that day.

We would have these awesome services at Sierra that ushered in the Spirit of Prophecy. I would always go up for prayer because I wanted more of God. Pastor Eddie would take his time to pray over and prophesy to as many people as possible. The church held about fifteen hundred people, and we may've had a thousand in attendance at the time. But he was patient, and he was sensitive to the Spirit of Lord.

He'd come to me in the line at the altar, and I was nervous. I'd never had anyone to speak directly to me from God. He looked at me and said, "Sister, you've only begun to scratch the surface." I cried and cried and cried and cried. God was going to do something with me after all. Hearing from God brought so much joy to my soul.

I would later receive the baptism of the Holy Spirit at one of our camp meetings, of which I was kind of afraid of because of all the stories I'd heard. One lady said that when she received the Holy Spirit it made her slide down under the pew. I'd watched other people "get the Holy Ghost," and run around the church – hollering a screaming. I definitely didn't want that. Shucks! I had a hard enough time lifting my hands and saying amen in church.

I didn't understand any of it because we didn't do that at the Kingdom Hall, and I knew I was not about to be sliding under pews and running around screaming and hollering.

"Lift your hands." The evangelist said.

"Do you want to receive the baptism of the Holy Ghost?"

"Yes, I do."

"Then lift your hands and let it flow." Huh? Let what flow? I could not comprehend what he was telling me to do. Then he laid his hands on me and began to pray.

"Yes Lord, I want it." I began to cry. As I cried - out came the sound of gibberish. Sounded like a baby trying to talk in whole sentences.

"Yes Lord, she's speaking in tongues." Everyone was so excited. The church went crazy, and I felt like I was having an out of body experience. Amazing.

We'd just come back from Woman Thou Art Loosed in Atlanta, Georgia and I was feeling revived.

We'd been back about four days and I go to the mailbox and there laid a check. It was from a 401K when I worked at Fruit of the Loom.

We needed that money. But that wasn't it. The next day I go to the mailbox and there laid a back child support check from child support enforcement. They'd picked Walter up over the weekend and the only way he could get out was to pay his arrears.

That was another, "Yes!"

I was so high in God by this time. It was as if He'd immediately began to move on my behalf. Then I remembered what Bishop Jakes said, "The heavens are open to you, and when you get back home things will not be the same." Wow! Wow! Wow!

Things were not the same. A reoccurring dream began to surface. It was a dream that I'd had for quite some time, but I just interpreted as spiritual and left it alone. In this dream, Jerry was always leaving me for another woman and I would be pleading with him asking him why was he doing this to me. He would always reply,

"This is what I want." I thought it meant that he was choosing the world over the church because I'd been trying to get him to go to church with me for the longest, but he always declined. This particular morning I'd had the dream. It was late August (approx. three weeks after the conference), and I'd got up as usual to prepare for work. Jerry was in the living room sitting on the sofa.

"Jerry, are you cheating on me?"
This was a question I'd asked several times before. As a matter of fact, every time I had the dream I would ask him and he would say no. But this time was different.
"Yeah, Tammie."

Oh my God! I ran into the bathroom and fell to my knees in tears. I couldn't believe the man that adored me so much was now seeing another woman. I'd gotten my act together, and was living as a Christian wife. Why would he choose now to cheat? We were buying our home. We'd come through some major financial woes. What was the problem? I finally gathered myself and walked back into the room where he was, picked up a broom and commenced to hitting him with.

If that wasn't enough I went into the kitchen and got a Pepsi and threw it at him. I was trying to hurt him with anything I could get my hands on. Again, he would never hit me back. In all the commotion, Chris woke up and came into the room. I will never forget the look on my baby's face (he was about 9), so I stopped fighting and went into the room to get dressed for work. Jerry stayed in the living room.

I was so hurt. When we got in the car for him to take me to work, I started again. I was filled with so much rage. I kicked him while he was driving. I hit him and then the ultimate – I spit on him. I was devastated. Later he told me that the worst thing you could do to a man was spit on him, and at that moment I knew our relationship would never be the same.

Jerry left that day and went back home with his parents. He took the only car we had at the time, so I was catching rides to work and to church. Until finally, Prophet Wayne, from church, offered me a car. It was a 1982 Toronado. That car got me around!

Prophet Wayne was a spiritual mentor to me. I'd taken several classes under him in the school of ministry and was especially enamored by his presence. He was a man that loved God. He would get up and prophesy and cry the whole time God was on him. Many looked up to him. He could walk into a room and the whole atmosphere would change. His presence alone brought correction. If you were doing wrong – his presence would make you want to repent and do right.

Jerry and I had bought several cars from him in the past, but I didn't realize that he was a Minister or Prophet until I began to go to Sierra. He would prophesy so heavy in that place, and the accuracy, good grief, was off the charts. I really grew fond of him over the years because he was genuine, and his ministry would be the initial introduction of the office of the prophet to me.

Chapter 10

EYES HAVEN'T SEEN

"What do you see?" Prophet Wayne asked.

"A huge eyeball. Looks like it is sitting on some bricks over a city." My gift was finally coming forth.

We were in the school of ministry studying prophecy and Prophet Wayne asked the above-stated question,

"What do you see?" At first, I hesitated to answer because it sounded real crazy. An eyeball on some bricks, really?? However, I finally mustered up the courage to raise my hand and answer. "I see a big eyeball sitting on some white bricks over a city." Everyone was amazed. I was seeing the watchmen's anointing. Prophet Wayne was, in fact, a watchman. He would see into the spirit, and in turn, warn us and give direction. Every Sunday and Wednesday I couldn't wait to see him walk through the doors of the church. He gave us so much hope in God.

When I was going through my separation, I called him. I was hurting so badly and needed some sound counsel.

"Prophet Wayne, my husband was cheating on

me, and now he is gone."

"Well Tammie, just keep your hands clean, and God will vindicate you."

"But I jumped on him and fought him."

"Tammie, don't you do anything else. Move out of the way and allow God to fight this battle for you."

"Okay, thank you."

Prophet Wayne was adamant about me keeping my hands clean, and I knew exactly what he meant.

"Keep your hands clean." Those words kept playing in my head. I had no desire to see anyone, but I did want some answers. "Who is she?" What does she have that I don't?" "Why would he leave us for someone else?" All these questions were surfacing, and I needed answers. Jerry worked from 7 p.m. to 7 a.m., and I'd gotten this bright idea that I would go to his job. He worked about 45 minutes from the house, so I left in plenty enough time to get there and sit and wait.

Tracey told me that the worse thing I could do was see them together, and she was right. It's about 6:30 p.m. and here he comes pulling in, but he is not alone. She is with him, along with her kids. At first, they didn't see me, but when they did I was getting out the car with a baseball bat. Jerry jumps out.

"Go home, Tammie!"

"No!" I cussed a little bit back then, so I used a few choice words as well. She was talking a lot of trash, but they (Jerry and Security) would not let me get close to her. Someone had called security and they escorted me off the premises. I was hurt even worse to know that she is driving our car. It was obvious that she was dropping him off for work.

How could Jerry do this? I'm saved now. I'm a better wife now – what happened?

As security was trying to get me back to my car (as you can imagine, I was very irate by this time), one of the guys said, "You didn't know this was going on."

"No, I didn't."

"Well, this has been going on for months."

"Huh?" I was somewhat confused.

"Yeah, he lives up here with her." The security guy replied.

"What! But he's been coming home."

"Well ma'am, they live together and everybody up here knows it."

I was outdone. I cried and screamed at God all the way home. For days upon days, I couldn't sleep. I'd been long stopped drinking alcohol, so my alternative was Ni-Quil – and I still could not sleep. I wouldn't measure it; I'd just turn it up, but to no avail. My mind was hurting. My soul was torn, but most of all my heart was broken. Jerry didn't love and adore me anymore. That fact alone tormented me day and night.

I tried to read my word, but it was not making much sense to me. So, I'd just lay there in depression. I'd go to work and barely function. Most of my days were spent in the bathroom crying. Reverend Beulah Legrande was a great support to me during that time. She told me that she had a dream about me before this happened. In her dream, she said that she was carrying me like a baby, and that's exactly what she did. She gave me scriptures to read. She would call me and pray with me. Whatever she felt led to do she would do it.

During one of our conversations, Reverend Legrande said, "I want you to learn to pray." Mind you, I'd been a part of the intercessory team at Sierra and thought I already knew how to pray. Little did I know, she was preparing me for the warfare that was to come. I knew I was called as an intercessor because God had confirmed that many times. But I'd never experienced this level of trial before.

About a month after Jerry left, I sat down and wrote out a prayer for our marriage. It was very detailed. I prayed that he would not love another woman and that he would only desire me. This is the kind of prayer that the soul prays. It was not Spirit led at all. Instead of praying such a selfish prayer, I should've been praying for him as a soul that God loves.

Jerry was not saved at the time, and that was one of the things that caused us to separate. He always felt I was a puppet for God. During one of my begging moments with him, he said, "I can't compete with God." I told him, "You don't have to compete with God." He said, "But that's your life, and I don't want to interfere with that." I couldn't understand his logic at the time, but later I realized that the breakup was a God thing.

Around Thanksgiving of that year, Jerry came back. It had almost been a full two months since he'd left, and I was very happy that he was coming home. Our family was back together, and things were soon to be back to normal – so I thought.

I'd lost about fifty pounds from fasting, and my resolve was to make the marriage work. However, I had a hard time trusting him. He would leave when he wanted to, and come back when he wanted to. But because I wanted my marriage so bad, I didn't put up a huge fight. I fussed, but it was nothing like before. I was fearful that he would leave again and never come back.

Christmas rolls around and I am headed to our annual Christmas party at church. Jerry looks at me and says,

"Um, where do you think you're going?" Jerry said.

"To our Christmas party at church, you wanna come?"

"No, and if this marriage is going to work, it's going to be all about me Miss Missy! All this running is going to cease."

My heart sank to my toes as I stood there looking at him. I'd already compromised so much in the past few months in order to get him back, now this? I did not want to compromise anymore.

I left for the party anyway. Somewhere between leaving the house and getting to the church – I talked myself out of it. "If I want my marriage to work I can't be at church all the time. I have to put him first."

The mental battle became so intense that instead of going to Sierra, to the Christmas party, I went to Belk and bought him some cologne. Then came back home, and gave it to him. I was so disgusted with myself. When you go against what you believe to please someone else you bring disrespect upon yourself. You've dishonored you, and so will everyone else.

Compromise is a self-defeating attribute that seeks to destroy your authenticity. The bible says, "Come let us reason together ..." Not, "Come and compromise what you believe." We can have everything going for us externally, but if we are not true to the God in us, then we have missed the mark. This is when idolatry is formed in the heart. God said, "I will have no other gods before me." Yes, he was my husband, but he was not my God, and the direction I was headed in – I would've made him just that.

HAPPY NEW YEAR! Everyone was so excited for the newness of a new year. We'd gathered that Sunday morning for worship at Sierra. I was so excited to be in church. I absolutely loved going there because it was so refreshing. I knew that if I could just get to the church, God would speak. And sure enough He did.

Pastor Jeannie, Pastor Eddie's wife, spoke a prophetic word to the congregation. I don't remember the totality of it, but it pertained to the spirit of compromise. I almost swallowed my tongue. I knew that I was living in a major state of compromise, but I justified it because of my Christian beliefs about marriage and divorce.

"It is God's will that husband and wife stay together." I rationalized in my mind that if I stayed home from church sometimes, step down off the choir and withdraw from the school of ministry – my marriage would get better.

"It was for the good of my marriage," I thought. All the while, I was miserable inside. When I was home, he was asleep because he had to work, so our relationship still suffered. Our communication was no better because I was too afraid to speak my mind – afraid he would leave.

One night I experienced God in a way that I'd never experienced Him before. I was lying in bed – not quite asleep – but drifting. I looked above me and there was no ceiling. I could see straight into the sky. The heavens opened, and Jesus began coming towards me. I could feel His presence so strong. I knew in my heart I was having a God encounter.

Shortly after the heavens opened I felt a hand fall upon my forehead. It began to press me down into the bed. The more the hand pressed - the farther Jesus went away. I couldn't move, but I could hear the Holy Spirit in me praying, and soon the hand let up and dropped on the bed. I could feel the thump as it hit. When I came to – I was shaken.

"What was that?"

"And whose hand was that on my head."

I got up and anointed my house, my children, and the man who was lying beside me – my husband. As I prayed about it, the Lord revealed that there was something coming between my relationship with Him. It was, in fact, my husband.

I woke up and told Jerry I could not do this anymore. He said ok, and he went back to his mother's house. I'd finally made the right decision. In that decision alone, I felt a peace that I'd never felt before.

"We need to fast and pray to see where your anointing is." She said. "Because with all the things that are happening – God has something for you to do."

Reverend Legrande was a very spiritual lady. She pastored a church in the city that was very successful. She shared so much with me. Things that helped me in my walk with God, and now, she wanted God to reveal to me what He'd anointed me to do. So, we went on a three day fast. On the second day – God showed up.

Again, the heavens opened before me. Out of them came these ginormous hands. It reminded me of a vision I'd had when I first got saved. In that vision, it was the same hands that came down for me. He wanted me to get into His hand. But this time – He opened His hands, and there lay His Word. His exact words to me were, "Teach My Word." It felt like thunder rumbling in my being. I knew it was God.

The next day I called Reverend Legrande and shared the news with her. She was so excited for me. She said, "That's just the beginning. There is more." She continued to teach me things, but eventually, God would move me on.

Chapter 11

HELLO QUEEN CITY

"Sister, God is going to move you, and it has something to do with your job."

My dreams were becoming more vivid, and the Lord was moving in some unusual ways. I was working for the Census bureau, and money was exceptionally tight. When Jerry left, so did his income. I was trying to make ends meet on $250 a week, but God was faithful to us.

Somewhere around March I began dreaming about moving. I kept seeing myself leaving Rockingham. I knew by the dream that I would be moving to a big city. When Sister Franklin gave me the prophetic word, "Sister, God is going to move you, and it has something to do with your job," I already knew it, but I didn't know where. I asked her if she knew if it would be in North Carolina, and she said, "Yes, it will be within the state." That was enough for me to begin praying about.

God eventually revealed to me that it would be in Charlotte. "Charlotte! Why can't I move to Raleigh?" I didn't have any interest in moving to Charlotte, I'd much rather move to Raleigh. But God knew best.

Now that I had the city, I just needed to know where in the city.

One day as I was praying and fasting, I heard the word "Bell" in my spirit. "Bell?" I'd been looking in the Charlotte Observer for days, so I quickly grabbed it and looked on the map in the classified ads. There it was – a street called Belhaven. I'd already dreamt of a white house with blue shutters, so now I knew where to look.

I called one of my friends, Roxanne and told her about it because they'd been praying with me about this move. She immediately responded, "We've got to go up there." Our faith was on ten thousand. The following Thursday Roxanne and I went to Charlotte and found the street. The only problem was what now? We drove around for a bit. There were a couple of housing developments on that street, but I couldn't wrap my mind around living in that area.

Who was I? I didn't deserve to live in such a nice area. I'd done nothing special to deserve such a blessing. So it was hard for me to receive it.

We finally found the house. It was a two-story home with four bedrooms. What? Are you kidding me? The home was beautiful! It was for sale, though. How in the world am I going to buy that? I had no money, no real job – nothing. Roxanne said, "Maybe they'll let you move in on a contract."

"What's that?"

I was so wet behind the ears. I didn't have a clue as to what she was talking about.

After finding the house and getting all the information on it, we returned to Rockingham. I was still in awe and unbelief. "God, you really want to give me this house?"

"Could this really happen for me? The whoremonger; the adulteress?" My past was still holding me hostage in my mind. I felt like I needed to earn God's goodness, and up until that point, I hadn't put in enough work for this. The favor of God was definitely upon my life. It had been for many years, but this topped everything.

A few days later I contacted the real estate agent and set an appointment to see the home. The next week, I returned to Charlotte. This house was a dream. Fireplace, one car garage, a bonus room. It was absolutely gorgeous. The agent gave me the listing price, and I almost passed out. I'm thinking "I will not be getting this house," but I did the application anyway.

Just as I'd thought. My credit was not good enough, and I did not qualify. Oh well, maybe this was not the home. I thought maybe God was going to erase some stuff just so I would credit qualify – but He didn't. I'm now packing up to leave the realtor's office, and I just happened to see the owners name on a document.

"Hmm, I'll call them myself."

I mean, what harm could it be in reaching out to the owners, after all – it was their house. As soon as I got back home I began looking up their name. I finally found their name and a telephone number. I took a deep breath and called them. A woman answers. She sounds to be in her early thirties maybe.

"Hi, my name is Tammie Ratliff, and I looked at your house today. I have some credit issues and could not qualify, but would you consider renting the home?"

I don't know where that came from, but they said yes. The woman on the other end of the phone said that if they couldn't sell it then they would lease it.

"Yes!" Now I have a chance. During the conversation, we made a connection. We talked about God and our lives. We were both excited. She'd stated that she was praying for a godly person to get their home. "Could she be talking about me?" Time would tell.

Working for the census bureau in Rockingham was rough – to say the least. We had to go around to people's homes and get a count of their household size. It seemed like I always got the very rural areas. Dirt roads and dogs. "Jesus, why me." Sometimes people would see us coming and purposefully go in the house and shut the door. It was no easy task.

The job was seasonal, so I tried to make the best of it. Near the end of the assignment, we had to attend a three- day training/wrap-up class. I was glad because I was tired of driving around. While in the class, the instructor said – get this – "If any of you are interested in moving to CHARLOTTE, they have some office positions coming open."

"Charlotte!" Wait a minute. Isn't that where God is moving me to? Didn't the prophecy say that the move would be "with my job?"

"Oh Lord, I can't take this." First, I find the house. Now, there are job openings in Charlotte with my current employer. Oh yeah, and those who worked the field got first dibs on the jobs. I was so overjoyed. The instructor told us how to apply, and as soon as I got home I was online applying for a position.

It had been a few days since I'd heard from the owners of the house, so I called them.

"Hi, do you have any offers on the house yet?"

"No. My husband and I are just going to lease it. His job needs him to transfer by June 15th, and we don't want to waste a lot of time waiting for a buyer."

"Ok, so what will be required to lease it?"

"We would need $1500 down, and a commitment of $1100 a month."

"Ok, I can do that." I didn't know how, but I had faith that God would come through. I did explain to them that I didn't have it at the moment, but I would get it.

"Alright, we will get you the lease agreement, and you just sign it and get it back to us with the money order."

It's happening! Everything is coming together. I called the Census bureau in Charlotte and found out that they'd received my application. It was just a matter of time now.

In the meantime, I was packing. I had boxes everywhere. I knew in my heart that this was a God move and that everything would fall in place like it should, even though I had no money at all.

After Jerry left, God was supernaturally taking care of us. People at church would walk up to me and say, "Sister, the Lord told me to bless you." It would always be hundred dollars or more.

I remember one Wednesday night at bible study we had amazing worship. The glory of God was H-E-A-V-Y! We were all on the floor in worship. I was near the back of the church between some pews in full-blown worship, it was such a solemn moment with the Lord, and I felt someone put something in my hand. It felt like a balled up piece of paper. I never looked up to see who or what it was; I just thought someone was slipping me a note.

After the presence lifted, we all got up one by one. There was still a lingering presence, so we just sat in it. It was so sweet in there. Eventually, I looked into my hand. It was not a piece of paper at all – it was a hundred dollar bill. Boy, did I cry. God made sure we didn't go without anything. At the end of the service, I got up and gave the testimony, still not knowing who put it in my hand.

About three weeks later, one of the deacons came up to me at the altar. He was a very astute man. He and his wife owned a dairy farm and were pretty well to do. He had tears in his eyes as he approached me.

"Sister, a few weeks ago, the Lord told me to sow a hundred dollars into your life. My wife handles the money, and I usually keep a hundred dollars stashed away in my wallet, but the Lord told me to give it to you."

"Thank you so much." I'd wondered for weeks who gave it to me.

He went on to tell me that he'd lost several

contracts, his wife was laid off, and money was tight. But after obeying God, and sowing that money into my life he received several new contracts, his wife was back to work – AND – when he arrived at church that morning someone gave him a check for $800. He was crying so badly, and so was I. He said, "I just want to tell you that you are good ground … you are good ground!" I felt the presence of God all over him. We embraced and cried for a few more minutes before returning to our seats.

All I could say was, "God, You are awesome!" I was so happy that someone had received a blessing from blessing me. It was moments like that, that assured me of God's faithfulness.

It is now May. In less than a month, the owners of the house would be moving to out west. I needed my job to come through, and I needed to get the money for the lease. I called the Census Bureau again, this time I spoke with a supervisor. She told me that she had a position for me, but she had to shut me down in Rockingham and bring me up in Charlotte.

Another week went by, no word. I called the owners to let them know where things stood. I was already fasting, so they joined in with me. I called the Census back. Still the paperwork had not been submitted.

"Alright, it's time to do something else."
I got in my car, drove to Charlotte, found the Census Bureau and asked to see a supervisor.

"How can I help you?"

"My name is Tammie Ratliff, and I applied for a position here. I have been talking with someone from your office who is supposed to be shutting my file down in Rockingham North Carolina so she can bring me on board up here."

"Ok, what is your social?" I gave it to her.

"I'll be right back." She comes back.

"Ok, here's what I found out. Your file is still open in Rockingham, but what I will do, myself, is go in and shut it down manually. Can you type?"

"Yes, I can."

"Ok, will you be able to start on June 15th?"

"Absolutely!"

She gave me all the particulars of the position and welcomed me aboard. Whew! "Thank You Jesus!" That was all I could say.

One more piece of the puzzle, the money. We are now in June. We are all fasting and praying for the money for the lease. Nothing is manifesting.

Friday, June 12th – the Lord instructs me to return all the items I'd borrowed from people. The first of which was an answering machine that Tracey had let me borrow to screen my calls. I was receiving a lot of hang-ups, and she thought it would be easy to see who was calling before I even attempted to answer the calls.

"Tracey, are you going to be home today?"

"Yeah, why?"

"The Lord told me to return all the things that I have that belong to someone else, and I have your answering machine."

"Ok, that's fine."

We chit chat a bit, and then she asks me the golden question.

"Do you have your money yet?"

"No, not yet. But I know it's coming."

She replied, "You got it."

I said, "Yeah, I know." I was speaking by faith, but she was speaking literally.

She said, "No, you got it because I have it."

"What?" My head was spinning.

"The Lord spoke to me and Charles, and told us to release it to you. Can you meet me at the Credit Union in about thirty minutes, and I'll give you the certified funds."

Look at God. She said He'd spoken about a week prior that they were to give it to me, but she was just waiting. There you have it. EVERYTHING was done!

The boys and I attended the owner's church that Sunday and gave them the money. After service, we all went out to eat and fellowshipped. At the last hour, God came through.

I had to get back to Rockingham because the next day I had to report to work in Charlotte. It took me about a week to get all my utilities on, so I couldn't stay at the house right away. But I did have the keys! Hallelujah to God!

Chapter 12

A FISH OUT OF WATER

This is a huge place, and the traffic is ridiculous! How can anyone be happy living in all this?

Every day for a week I commuted from Rockingham to Charlotte for work. The drive wasn't bad until I got into Charlotte. The boys were out for the summer, and between my mom and Jerry's mom, they were well taken care of. Finally, all of my utilities are on, and we can move in. We were happy. But to be honest, I didn't know how I was going to pay all of my bills, but I believed God.

One of the first things I did when I got to Charlotte was attend Pastor Robin Gould's church, Victory Christian Center. I'd watched him on TV almost every morning since I got saved, so I knew that I would grow there. Things are going great. A good friend of mine, Lisa, surprised me with some much-needed furniture, so I didn't have to go in debt right away. The boys were in school, and things were finally settling down.

"Ring, Ring"

"Hello." In my curious George tone.

"Hey baby, I heard you moved to Charlotte. You want me to come see you?" Oh God! It was my kryptonite – Anthony.

"Uh, yeah." I really wanted to see him and show off my new house. I knew I shouldn't have, but I felt like I couldn't help it. He was my weakness, and the enemy knew it.

Almost every weekend he would come up, but only at night. I didn't want the boys to know that he was there. So he'd come in at about midnight, and leave before day.

Hereto again, it was all about the sex. I beat myself up so much about it because God had done some miraculous things in my life, and this is how I would repay him? (Sigh) I was so weak when it came him. Man, that struggle was real.

"They are opening positions with the federal government, and we get to apply internally." Jaleesa had some inside information and was spreading the news. Whew! This would be the financial increase that I needed.

I requested the package, and it came in about two weeks. It was the necessary paperwork to apply for the job. I took the papers out only to glance at them. It was a lot of paperwork to fill out so I laid it aside until later. Later never came.

It was Monday, the day of my interview. Anthony had been there all night, and I needed to be downtown by 9 a.m. I think he left about seven, and I was tired. So, after I got the boys off to school, I laid back down.

"Oh God! It's 8:25." I jumped up, put on some clothes, grab my envelope (papers still not filled out), and run out the door.

"Lord please don't let me be late." I distinctively remember the paperwork saying, 'If you are a minute late, you forfeit your interview'. I had to make it downtown to the federal building in about 15 to 20 minutes – impossible. My heart was pounding because I knew this was an opportunity of a lifetime.

I get to the building at 9, but I didn't factor in that they had to scan me, check my purse and do all that government security stuff. I'm finally at the interview room, it's 9:05. The interviewer says, "Ma'am I can't let you in."

"Oh no! Please" I started to cry. As I am walking away, he comes out and says, "Come on back. I will let you in this time."

"Thank you! Thank You! Thank You!"

I go in and sit down. He then asks for my paperwork. I look at him like a deer in front of headlights.

"I haven't filled it out completely sir."

"Ok, let me see." He looks at the blank forms.

"You haven't even filled in your name, ma'am."

"I didn't have time, and I thought I could do it when I got here."

"No ma'am, that's why we send it to you, Have a good day."

I was asked to leave. That was one of the worst days of my life. An opportunity missed because of my selfishness. An opportunity missed because I'd taken advantage of God's goodness. God had set me apart, and opened great doors for me, and I couldn't even deny my flesh, and see it through. I'd lost focus, and was so off track.

I was no longer attending Victory Christian Center regularly. My focus was so off that I would go when I felt like it. Some Sunday's I would go to John P. Kee's church, just to be going somewhere. Everything was so hard. I couldn't even pray – I felt so far from God. It's funny because, after that incident at the Federal Building, Anthony didn't come up anymore. I'd been swindled out of my blessing. The enemy knew God was up to something with me, and he had to stop it as quick as possible. I'd gotten so distracted that I didn't even notice.

We've just received notice that we were being laid

off. What will I do now?

"I know, I'll start my own business," and that is exactly what I set out to do.

During my marriage, I opened my own alterations shop in downtown Hamlet. The space was located in the legendary Coltrane's Blue Room. It was a landmark location dedicated to the jazz musician John Coltrane. I did very well and knew that Charlotte would be a great place to start back up.

So, I rented a small space in Salon Central on Freedom Drive and began doing alterations. Nevertheless, bills are getting further and further behind.

The owners were calling about the rent. But what do I tell them? I'm not working?

Fear had taken a hold of me once again. Instead of talking with them – I ignored their calls, and when I finally did answer they were furious. Because I had no good explanation, I simply said to them, "Do what you have to in order to save your house." I didn't feel that I deserved God's help or anyone else's for that matter. I'd messed up royally this time.

A few months later, we were evicted, and went to stay with one of the ministers at the church that I'd been attending for the past two months. Minister Alex and I knew each other from work (the census office).

We talked a lot about God and the prophetic. That was right down my alley. That was the one thing I missed from Sierra – the prophetic flow. So joining myself to this ministry seemed right.

The first day I attended this church I came home and had a dream:

I was in a small canoe-like boat. I stuck my hand in the water and a snake bit me. My hand began to scale over. I quickly took my hand out of the water and began to pray. My hand was then healed.

I didn't know what this meant at the time - until I had yet another dream:

I was in this house, and I left the living room to explore the house. As I looked in this one particular room, there was a Dr. who looked like a Dr. Jekyll type (Mad scientist). He was putting a dead woman together with other people's body parts. I saw him screwing her hands on, then her legs. The dream was so real I could smell the rottenness of the bones. His intention was to present her as his wife. When I saw this, I began to run through the town, telling everyone that this woman that he was about to bring out was not his wife. It was a dead woman that he'd put together.

It was the church. The church that I was a part of was a dead work that he was trying to resurrect through the gifts of others. I knew it was something fishy about it. The pastor actually came to work at the Census Bureau for a couple of weeks before we were laid off. Minister Alex had told him of our conversations, and how prophetic I was, so he wanted me to come to his church. He'd sent messages before that I needed to be covered under a prophet, but I was a bit hesitant. So I guess his coming to work with us was his way of "making it happen."

In my innocence and sense of displacement, I finally agreed. After I joined, the pastor quit working at the Census Bureau. In hindsight, his assignment was to come get me. He had this idea that he would groom me (That's what the scales represented in the dream), but it was not of God.

My brother, Shawn, was living with me now, and we'd moved into an apartment. Brother George lived in the same complex and became very good friends with my brother. They hung out and spent quite a bit of time together, but with the revelation that God had given me I couldn't stay there. It was time to call the pastor to tell him I was leaving.

When I told him I was leaving the ministry, he went on a cuss fest. He told me I was crazy, and that no one will ever allow me in their pulpit. I was deeply hurt and confused. One minute you say I am full of wisdom, and the next you call me crazy. These were very damaging words for a woman with low self-esteem. I had a gift, but I had no identity. I had no confidence. I was fearful, full of guilt, and still struggling with feelings of unworthiness. Now, you tell me I'm crazy. His words immobilized me. I wasn't sure of where I was going or anything. Losing the house and being out of the will of God was crippling enough, and his deadly words only added insult to the already injured.

After that, Shawn attempted to connect with Brother George, but to his surprise, was turned away. I asked Shawn why, but he didn't know. So, I took it upon myself to find out.

I went over to Brother George's house, and he was very rude to me. The word had gotten out about the conversation the pastor and I had, and no one was talking to us. Brother George even went so far as to slam the door in my face and told me to get away from his door.

"All of this because I'd left the ministry. At least I did it correctly. Some people just leave." I yelled through the door. I was livid!

Shortly after this incident, I was on the phone talking with one of my uncles trying to make sense of everything. I shared my ordeal with him, along with some other things, and his suggestion was that I go back to New Life (Pastor Kee's church).

The first night I went, he preached from Galatians 3:1, "O foolish Galatians, who hath bewitched you, that you should not obey the truth," That's all I needed to hear. The word was corrective but sobering. I knew then that out of desperation for a spiritual father, I'd fallen prey to yet another trick of the enemy. The Father had shown me the truth many times, but I chose to follow the way of man, which opened the door to deception.

I remained at Pastor Kee's church for about a year. The banner of his church was so befitting for my 'then' state. It was definitely a place "Where the Healing Begins." And man-o-man did I need to be healed.

While at New Life, God would slowly rebuild me. It was truly a breath of fresh air. My brother and I got involved in the different events and became "Partakers." That is what Pastor Kee calls the people of the ministry instead of members.

Although I didn't have the confidence to really

sing, I joined the praise team, and the mass choir. I would sing at home all the time, and thought it would be good to exercise my vocals, and glean from the more experienced.

Pastor Kee is a master vocalist. He belted out tunes like it was nothing. Especially that high-pitched note he would hit when he was transitioning a song. The first time he did it I looked around to see who was singing it. It sounded like a woman, but it was him. They were always singing good, upbeat and worshipful music.

The first summer there, I tried my hand at his "New Artist Showcase," during the VIP conference. Let's just say, "I flopped in a major way." I got on that stage and forgot the words to Alabaster Box by Cece Winans. I'd sang it at Sierra before I left and did very well. I think it was because when I sang at Sierra, I was going through my break-up with my ex-husband, and my emotions were raw. But at New Life, it was awful. How do you flop in front of John P. Kee. I know Pastor Kee was saying, "Bless her heart – she tried." I couldn't wait to get through that song so I could get back to my seat. I wanted to leave, but I gathered my embarrassment and stayed for the rest of the night.

The VIP went on for a week. There were guest

speakers like Paul Morton; Brian Moore; Rance Allen and many other names. I was new to that level of ministry, so I was not familiar with many of the speakers at that time.

Somewhere around midweek, I looked up and there was Brother George, and a few of the other members from my previous church, in the service. They all were very cordial. I think brother George was there to sing in the showcase that night. He had an awesome voice.

When I was in their ministry, he led praise and worship and tried to help me find my voice, but I was too afraid to really let go and let God take over. I had a good voice, but I had no voice control. I knew nothing about singing – other than singing around the house.

After the service was over, Brother George came over to me.

"Sister, I am so sorry for shutting you and your brother out."

He went on to explain to me that shortly after I left, the church was dismantled. The Pastor closed the doors, and they all went their own separate ways. I was not surprised because shortly after I left I dreamt about them.

Dream: They were all walking with backpacks on like wanderers.

In the natural (real life), they'd all come from Washington State with him to start the ministry. A few of them sold their homes. They gave up good jobs and everything, and now they have nowhere to go. Brother George was very regretful and wished he'd gone in another direction. He'd wanted to go to Alabama and get married, but listening to the counsel of the pastor – He didn't. He told me that I was a woman of God, and he was so sorry about the things we had to go through.

What a relief! God will vindicate you. Just hold your peace, and let Him fight the battle. After I left their ministry, I never looked back. As I prayed for that pastor, God gave me another dream:

Dream: He and his wife started another church in a school. He looked so vibrant. His demeanor had really changed, and his approach to me was that of a very humble man. They greeted me with great joy.

Interpretation: God was going to restore his ministry, but he was going to have to go through a season of humbling.

The man whom I saw in the dream was nothing like the man that I encountered. The man I experienced was very arrogant. He had a strong spirit of pride on him. At first, I thought that this was the way a prophet should carry himself. But after really studying the word, I came to understand that God hates pride. We should never think so much of ourselves that we feel it's ok to put other people down.

Chapter 13

TEN TOES UP WITH TEARS IN MY EYES

"I've been waiting on you." These were the first words I would hear from the pastor of that church.

It was Wednesday night bible study, and I'd been told about this particular church by a couple of people that came into my shop. Although I was still at New Life, I was curious about going to this church.

I walk in and sit on the last row. The pastor is up preaching, and now it is time for the altar call. He is moving prophetically and begins to call out different issues. The Spirit of the Lord is pulling at my heartstrings, but I am too afraid to go up. I was in yet another storm, and I was in need of a word of direction, but I could not work up enough nerve to leave my seat.

Finally, my feet begin to lead me right down to the altar, and I am now standing in front of the man of God.

"I've been waiting on you. You are one of the ones God was talking to about bringing stability to your life." Wow, how did he know? After losing the house, nothing was sure to me anymore. I still carried a lot of guilt. I'd drug my children from pillar to post and needed some sense of direction for my life, and this pastor spoke directly to my circumstances.

I began going to the Wednesday night bible study and later joined the church. God was putting my life in order. A few bumps and bruises here and there, but I was finally in the ministry God had assigned me to. New Life helped me heal, but Temple is where I would grow and see God in a whole other light. A greater light.

Because of my love for singing I immediately joined the choir. After meeting with the pastor, it was his suggestion that I also join the prayer ministry. Ms. Willie Mae was the leader at that time, and boy could she call down fire from heaven. Sitting under her was more of a blessing than I knew. At first we didn't set horses, but later she would become one of my closest friends.

One of the guys that told me about Temple was also in pursuit of me, and would soon become my boyfriend. I'd met him when I moved over on the Westside of Charlotte. We hit it off, and before I knew it – I was ten toes up with tears in my eyes … again! Oh my goodness, how in the world was I caught up again?? 2 years had passed since my stint with Anthony, and I was feeling pretty good about my celibacy, and now this. I'd remained focused on managing my life. I purposefully did not enter into a relationship because I knew it would distract me, and after Anthony I could not afford any more distractions.

I'd met a guy who was doing plays, through a mutual friend, and began traveling with them. I'd also been singing at McDonald's Cafeteria on Sunday's to strengthen my voice as well, so I really did not have time for a relationship. But this one seemed so right.

The relationship was on again and off again because I didn't want to be sleeping with him. I wanted the relationship, but I remembered what happened to me the last time, and I did not want to go through that again. Nevertheless, I continued on with the sexual aspect of the relationship.

WORD OF WISDOM: The sexual struggle in the church is a real struggle. Many women today desire a mate, but they don't want to become just a bed buddy. Once you get entangled it is hard to come out. I know, I've been there many times – while in ministry. But my words to you ladies is this: Don't allow yourself to be condemned. God created us with the desire for a man, so it is in us to long for male companionship. However, we should never get comfortable in a sexual relationship outside of a covenantal commitment. There is too much at stake here. Once you give your body away – you become soul tied to that person. You begin to yearn for them and eventually consumed by them. When you are soul-tied you can sense their presence without even looking around. The tie is so strong that you can even know when they are with someone else. That is a powerful bond! So be careful who you allow yourself to become "one" with.

"Lord, I am so sorry. Please help me." This was my cry on a regular basis. I thought I was strong enough to handle the relationship, without sex, but it was obvious – I couldn't. I felt trapped. I felt that I would never be able to stop fornicating with this man. But that was not what was holding me. This man also took very good care of me. He made sure I had what I needed. He held me when I needed to be held, and supported me when I needed support, and to add icing to the cake - he was a minister.

I wanted to get married, but he didn't. He kept saying that he wasn't ready for marriage again. I accepted it but was still struggling with the relationship.

I finally moved to the opposite side of town into another house. It was not as big as the first one, but it was nice. I invited my boyfriend over once but knew in my mind that I had to end the relationship. My way of doing this was simply not answering his calls. He couldn't remember where the house was so he couldn't just pop up. I knew it was harsh, but that was the only way I knew to end it for real. He was still attending my church, but I purposefully wouldn't talk to him after service. As a matter of fact, I would rush out after it was over just to avoid him. I really needed to be free from the mental battle that came along with that relationship. By this time, it was not just the sex; he was also seeing other women.

When I finally got out of that relationship, I went right back to being my old religious self. Condemning everyone. Although I'd been caught up a few times myself, it didn't soften my heart towards other people's struggle – that, would come later in life. I felt like everybody who was doing wrong was going to hell. God had given me a few spiritual experiences and I thought I'd reached the pentacle of my Christian walk.

SIDENOTE: This is what happens when you have low self-esteem, carry unworthiness, guilt, shame, and rejection. You have no real identity so you cling to your gifts, which in many cases cause us to get puffed up in pride.

Yes, I had my struggles and failures, but I was still not like "those people." There were many times that I felt like no one could hear God but me. How lame is that? Although I had a strong gift of discernment, my heart wasn't right. When your heart isn't right – you will, without a doubt, hurt people.

Months went by and I was elevated in ministry. This really swelled my head. I felt privileged. It was nothing that I would ever voice, but inside I was feeling like someone real special. I'd go to church and come home like a good Christian. I displayed all the outward signs of a holy lifestyle. I can't say that I was blatantly prideful, but I will say that I felt a sense of elitism. "I'm a part of the in-crowd." I really thought that was the place to be. But the truth of the matter is this: The higher the level – the greater the devil. Are you ready?

As I am functioning in this new capacity, I begin to receive a lot of attention – from men, and yeah, you guessed it – here we go again. This time it was strictly sexual. It was a sexual relationship like I'd never known.

"Oh my God!" I'd been doing so well! But here again, when you have a hole in your soul - sex becomes the medication that anesthetizes the pain.

Even though it didn't last long, there was still that little something down on the inside that made me feel good to know that a man of this caliber wanted me – even if it was for nothing more than sex.

But this time I was noticing a change in me. My desire to be wanted was not as strong as it had been. After the initial encounters, I began to recognize my yet empty soul and didn't want to feel empty anymore.

Far too many of us enter into and remain in unhealthy relationships trying to satisfy that emptiness. Who cares if they lie to us. Who cares if they verbally and/or physically abuse us. Who cares if it's just for the sex. Who even cares if they see other women, as long as you get your time, right? Wrong! These are the mentalities of a broken soul – and God wants to heal that.

God wants you to know that you are valuable. He also wants you to know that you do not have to settle and accept unacceptable behavior just to have someone in your life. You may have to go it alone for a season, but even the rewards of being alone are great. You finally get to know you! You finally get the chance to get clear about why God allowed you to be born. He very well may have created you to be someone's wife (the strength of her husband). But at least you would have had the time to find that out when you go solo for a while.

Relationships are wonderful (please don't misunderstand me), however, we can't enter into them because we have a need. We must have something to offer that relationship other than our brokenness. It's not fair to the other person.

Some people are simply addicted to sex. That's a whole other book. But for the most part, many are simply looking for validation. People simply want to know that they matter to someone.

Let me put a pin right there!

YOU MATTER to God. You are someone special in the eyes of our heavenly Father. There is no amount of sexual activity that can anchor your soul like being in a relationship with God.

It has taken me many years to get this, but now that I have it – I have it.

Repeat after me:

Affirmation #1
I Have Value Because Of Who Lives In Me, And Not

Just Anyone Can Put Their Hands On Me.

Affirmation#2
I Have A Divine Purpose In God, And Not Just Anyone Can Be Connected To Me.

Affirmation#3
I Am God's Handy-work, Created For Good Works, And My Body Is The Temple Of The Holy Spirit.

Chapter 14

LIFE AT THE LAKE

The boys were gone. Christopher was off to college and Matrix had left to go live with his dad, and I had embarked upon another phase of my life.

"Roommate Wanted." That was the header for the ad on craigslist. I'd always wanted to live on the water and this was a great opportunity to do that. It was actually a two story house on Lake Norman that was converted into two separate living spaces. My living quarters was on the lower level and my landlord and his girlfriend lived upstairs.

The view from my bedroom was impeccable. I could roll over and watch the sun rise and set right on the water from my sliding glass door. It was so serene.

I was working with Keller Williams Realty as a Real Estate Agent and had been to Lake Norman on numerous occasions showing property. It was a place that I didn't think I would ever be able to afford, but God changed that.

I began to meet some really cool and well-to-do people. It was a life that I'd only dreamt of living. Taking personal boat rides over to different restaurants on the lake; going to dinner parties; being privy to the various lifestyles – this life was bliss.

I was still attending church and working with the pastor, so this experience afforded me balance.

Jerome, the guy I was leasing from, had become a very good friend of mine and he shared a lot of property leasing information with me. He allowed me to work in his office part time leasing homes all over Charlotte.

"Jerome, can you come get me, my car just put me down."

"Yeah, where are you?"

"I'm downtown near the Amtrak station."

It took him all of ten minutes to get to me. He had my car towed to a nearby mechanic station and we went home. It was a Friday evening so I didn't have to worry about going into Charlotte for a couple of days, so I just relaxed.

A few days before my car broke down my mom called and told me that I needed to sow $7 dollars to my church. I thought it was odd, but I did it anyway. I'd also received a prophetic word from a close friend that I was about to get a truck. How? I had no idea.

"Tammie, can you come up here, please?" It was Jerome calling.

"Be there in a minute."

His girlfriend had just come from the BMW dealership where she'd purchased a cute little silver BMW.

"What's up?"

"Sherry just bought a new car, and I was wondering if you would like to take up payments on her truck?"

It was a 2005 Mitsubishi Montero Sport.

"What are the payments?"

"Don't worry, they are affordable."

We went over the particulars and he handed me the keys. Wow! Look at God. Now here's the kicker – Jerome was a self-professed atheist, but he respected me as a Christian.

Once there was a situation that arose and he called me into his office and asked me to do that "thing" that I did.

"What thing Jerome?"

"You know, pray to your God, and ask Him what should I do about this situation."

Jerome knew that I prayed and had dreams that were accurate, and although he said he didn't believe in God he trusted the God in me.

Sure enough, I prayed and God answered. I went back to Jerome and told him what he should do in the situation. It was something that he was not willing to do, so he ended up getting the bad end of the deal.

His attachment to me had grown a great deal and I could sense it. When it was time for me to travel with my pastor or do something at the church, Jerome would find extra work at the office for me to do.

One year the church was going to Chicago for a gathering. I'd worked extra hard to make a little more for this upcoming trip. Jerome knew I was leaving for a few days and needed my money, but he was nowhere to be found. I called and I called – no Jerome. Fortunately I was able to borrow some money from some friends to hold me over while I was in Chicago, but boy was I pissed.

When I got back I went straight to the office to confront Jerome.

He says, "Tammie hi, how was your trip?"

"My trip was wonderful!" I could see the sarcasm written all over his face, so instead of showing him how upset I was I went along with his game.

"How was your weekend Jerome?"

"It was good."

"Oh, ok. That's great." Still holding my composure.

He then says, "By the way I noticed you didn't get your check before you left."

"Yeah, I had a lot of running to do and didn't have

time to come by here."

As I am talking I look over in my box and there was my check. I'm thinking, "This man is crazy." I've never liked to be toyed with by anyone, and he was no exception. He claimed it was there before I left, but I knew better. He was playing games with me.

Soon after, I decided to work more with selling real estate rather than leasing. I'd obtained my Brokers license and I wanted to connect with a well-known firm and tap more into brokerage.

I resigned from my job with Jerome and signed on with ERA. Jerome was not happy and he did not make my transition easy. He demanded the truck back and wrote a letter to the Real Estate Commission in Raleigh to have my license revoked for stealing his truck.

This allegation, of course, was a bold faced lie, and fortunately I had evidence to prove it. Needless to say, I fought the accusations and won. He'd also pulled my credit and my background history and sent it to my pastor's office. I guess he thought it would make him not want to work with me any longer. But that didn't work either.

As you could imagine, I could no longer live in the house, so I bowed out gracefully. It forced me to get an extended stay at the Howard Johnson, but at least I was not on the streets of Charlotte.

Chapter 15

".... ANOTHER BABY"

The Howard Johnson was not the best place to be, but it sufficed for the moment.

In between working the real estate I took on part time jobs through the temp agency.

"Tammie, we have a position we think you would be very suited for, but it's in Salisbury. They are offering $13 an hour. Would you be willing to take it?"

"Let them know that I would need at least $16 an hour to take that drive."

"Alright, we will submit your counter offer and call you back. Cross your fingers because they do not usually go up that much for an admin assistant."

For some reason, I was not even concerned with whether or not they would accept the offer. I wanted the job, but I knew that I could not settle for $13 hr. "Tammie! They accepted! Can you come by the office and finish the paper work?"

"Yes, I will be there shortly. Thanks."

Working in real estate means "if you don't sell a house – you don't eat," so I was grateful to have this job. The market was changing and so was the economy, and to work in real estate meant you had to work extremely hard as well as long hours. Call it lazy, but I was just not willing, and besides I was not managing my finances well enough to be an entrepreneur.

Nationwide insurance was about a 45minute drive one way. After Jerome took the truck I found myself renting a car by the week. That got really expensive so when my money ran out Joanne would let me borrow her car.

She was a true friend indeed. As I was being elevated at church she stood by me. A lot of people didn't understand how I was being elevated so quickly so I didn't have a huge support system. Had they just took the time to talk to me they would have known that it was just as new to me as it was to them.

My pastor saw who I was in God, and he did everything the Lord instructed him to do concerning me, and I moved with it. But the problem was – I did not remain humble in it.

Everyday traveling 85 North was a joy. I would get up at 5 am, pray and hit the road. But one morning I decided to start sending out a "Quote of the Day." For two mornings straight I sent the quote out to people at church. Then on the third morning I heard the Holy Spirit say, "Morning Deposit." The more I meditated on it the clearer it became. By the time I finished writing that morning, the name had become "The A.M. Deposit." The quotes turned into mini-essays.

"O God, thou art my God; early will I seek thee: my soul thirsteth for thee, my flesh longeth for thee in a dry and thirsty land, where no water is;" Psalm 63:1

This became the theme scripture for the daily deposits. A new baby was born. I'd tapped into a gift that the Lord had spoken to me about in the late nineties.

I was sitting on my couch and He began to speak to me about my purpose, and one of the things He said was that I would write many books and articles and travel all over the world. At the time, I could not see how that would happen, but God did it!

My mornings were everything to me. I would get up, take a shower and sit down and begin writing. Many of the deposits came from a simple phrase or scripture. It has always been a habit to ask the Holy Spirit, "What is it that God wants His people to know," and from there He would begin to speak. I was just the holder of the pen.

Soon, I began receiving exciting feedback from many of the people at the church. This inspired me all the more to share. Most of the times though the deposit was really a way of me encouraging myself. After the whole fiasco with Jerome, and now I am living in a hotel – I needed some strength. I never told anyone where I was living because, of course, I was ashamed. But the ultimate happened, and it just about made me lose my mind.

Chris was coming home for summer break from college. Where would he go? I had no other choice but to tell him where I was staying. I was humiliated for him. It was not the norm for a child to see their fully capable parent living in a hotel. I know it broke his spirit because it broke mine. He endured with me, though, and when the summer was over he returned to school.

Here I was again, over the prayer ministry, being elevated at church but living beneath my privileges. It was rightly so a place called "Adullam."

Adullam was situated in the Valley of Elah. There was a cave there that David retreated to after running from Saul known as "The Cave of Adullam." It would be in this place that David would begin his Kingship. It was in that cave that many would come to him to be led by him.

"And everyone that was in distress, and everyone that was in debt, and every one that was discontented, gathered themselves unto him; and he became captain over them ..."

The power of this text is that the cave was located in a low place (valley), but the cave itself was sitting on a hill in that low place. How about that. I was in a high place while in a low place.

Side note: buy the book! It will bless your soul.

"The A.M. Deposit, A 40 Day Compilation of Writings From the Cave of Adullam."

Chris was gone back to school and I was determined to find me a place to live. I'd been paying roughly $400 a week there, and things were getting tight.

My credit was shot from the evictions so getting an apartment was not an option. I ended up obtaining a room in a house with four other ladies. It was nice, and it was not far from the ERA office.

While I was there I continued to send out my daily deposits, and God was restoring me once again.

When I first got there I was introduced to everyone in the house except for one young lady who was away visiting family. Once she returned we met, but she didn't seem too friendly.

Rosalyn was a go-getter. She was focused on her life and did not have time for foolishness. At first, I kept it on a "Hi" and "Bye" basis with her. But over the next few months of us being there we would get to know each other a little better.

A lady at church had given me a little BMW, and I was driving it to death. That little car was no joke. One thing I can say is that God has always taken care of me.

Chapter 16

ON TO BIGGER THINGS

I'd dreamt of this place a few years prior, and now I'm here.

Her name was Christy. I'd met her through a mutual friend, and we hit it off right away.

I'd had a dream about this Caucasian lady who was dealing with a particular issue, and in the dream the Lord had me ministering to her. Upon waking, I was telling our mutual friend about the dream and she said, "O God Tammie, that's Christy. You need to tell her this."

As I began to share this information with her she began to cry. She shared with me some of the things she's prayed about and my dream answered something specific for her.

"Can you come out here? I have to meet you." She asked.

"I guess," I replied. I was beyond shocked that she would ask to meet me.

"Don't worry about anything. I'll pay for it. You just tell me when you want to come and I'll buy the ticket." She continued.

"Umm, ok." I agreed to go.

Within two weeks of that conversation, I was in Dallas Texas.

"Hi, Tammie!" Christy was one of the prettiest white girls I'd ever seen.

"Hi Christy, how are you." It was if we'd always known each other.

"How was your flight?"

"A little shaky, but other than that it ok."

"Well, get ready to fly again because we are flying into San Antonio tomorrow. A friend of mine is doing a play and we are going to support him."

"Ok." Is this really happening? The generosity of this woman is unbelievable.

The next day we fly into San Antonio. What a rough flight. I'd never flown Southwest Airlines and was not in a hurry to do it again.

"This place is beautiful!" I thought.

We stayed at the Hilton on the River Walk, and what an experience it was. Christy was determined to show me a good time. That night we went to the play and flew back to Dallas the next day. My trip was planned for a week but turned into two weeks. During that week, Christy literally spoiled me. She took me to many dinners. Introduced me to friends and neighbors. It was awesome.

The time had come to leave.

"So, when are you moving back?"

"I don't know. Let me pray about it."

There really was nothing to pray about. A few years prior the Lord had shown me in a vision during prayer that I would go to Texas and get a very good job – but it would only last for six months. So I knew that this was that open door.

"I can get you on at the University."

"Ok. Let me get back and take care of some things and I will come back." That was in May of 2007. On June 29th, a month later, I was in my car headed to Texas. Seventeen and a half hours straight I drove. Christy had sent me the money for gas, food, and lodging, but I just wanted to get there, so I drove it straight through.

A quarter till eleven I arrived at her home. I was so tired, I slept for a day and a half. My legs felt like pure spaghetti.

When I finally came to (woke up), Christy handed me a couple of hundred dollar bills and said, "Here, go buy you some clothes." She was working on getting me on at the University and she wanted me to look my best.

I drove around the town for several days just getting familiar with everything. I loved being there.

Christy's home was located in a little community similar to Birkdale in Huntersville, North Carolina. Again, I was among the affluent.

"They put a freeze on the jobs at the school," Christy said.

"What! Are you serious?" I was feeling like I'd made a mistake going there.

"Yeah, I found out today."

"Ok God. I know you didn't bring me out here for this. What am I suppose to do?" It has only been a week, I couldn't turn right back around and drive back to North Carolina.

"We'll just have to blast your resume." Christy was so full of faith. That's what I loved about her.

I began flooding every online job market I could. I even went to the temp agency there. I was going to stay and see what God had in store for me.

"Ring! Ring!"

"Hello."

"Yes, may I speak with Tammie Ratliff?"

"This is she."

"Hi Tammie, I am calling on behalf of Gap Inc. We have a position that you may be interested in. Can you come in for an interview on Wednesday at 1:00 p.m.?"

"Yes, I can."

"Ok. Just make sure you bring a copy of your resume with you."

"Alright, thanks."

"Yes honey! I'm going to get this job." I was so confident that I would get it. The position was as a project coordinator in Gap's corporate real estate division and having a background in real estate I just knew I could do it.

The day of my interview I wore the suit that the prayer ministry had bought me for my birthday. It was my power suit. I felt corporate in it.

I get to the building, and my goodness it is huge. I find the office that the interview is to be held and I go in and wait for them to call me back. The receptionist then motions for me to come with her. As I enter the room there sit no one person but THREE.

"O My Goodness! Lord be with me."

All of them were looking directly at me as I walked in and sat down. Sweat was pouring, already. Whelp! There went my confidence. The VP off construction begins to interviewing process. I was so intimidated. This man was in his early sixties, very distinguish and well spoken. His name was Tom.

The interview lasted about thirty minutes or so, and boy was I glad to get out of there.

"Oh well, I guess I'll keep looking." Those were

my thoughts because they were looking for someone with a degree – of which I did not have, so I continued my search.

"Ring! Ring!"

"Hello."

"Hi, is this Tammie?"

"Yes, it is."

"Hi, this is Kim from Gap, how are you?"

"Hi, Kim! I'm fine, how are you?"

"I'm fine. Listen, I've got good news – you got the position. Can you start in the morning?"

"Absolutely!" It had been four days since the interview and I really had given up on it.

"Breathe Tammie, breathe." That's what I kept telling myself. I had to pull over because I was driving at the time, and the news had taken my breath away.

"Christy, guess what girl? I got the job at Gap!" She was happier than I was." Of course, we went out to eat to celebrate.

My first day at work they gave me my office. You hear that – an office – not a cubicle. With a BIG door! I can't even begin to describe to you how I felt. I was nervous the first few days because I had to learn their software, processes, and procedures, and most of all – work with Tom.

I felt like a fumbling idiot because he was a very organized man.

"Why does he need me?" Because of my feelings of inadequacy, all I wanted to do was go in my office, shut the door and do my work. But it was not that easy. My work consisted of assisting the VP of construction – Tom.

Eventually, I got comfortable in that environment and Tom began taking me on trips with him. "My God, what did I do to deserve this?"

Christy had given me a huge piece of Ralph Lauren luggage, and I was just all sorts of beside myself. This time I was truly humbled. I didn't really know what I was doing, and my only goal was to give my best.

Six months had come and gone. I was really enjoying Dallas and did not want to leave. In fact, I ended up staying another three months. But in March of 2008, I put in my resignation. As Tom stated on my last day, it was "one of the saddest days of my life."

I had to obey God and return to Charlotte. My tenure was up, and it was time to get back in place. The Lord spoke to me and told me, "I brought you here to renew your strength."

Before I left for Texas, I'd become weary in ministry. I'd stepped down from the prayer ministry and needed a break. I know what you may be thinking, "If you are called to ministry, it's not an option to take a break," and I hear you, however, I was very weary and offended – and God knew what I needed … A Break.

Two weeks before I was to return, I went to the gynecologist for my annual check-up. While there, I asked for a prescription of ibuprofen for arthritis in my hip. I'd been diagnosed with osteoarthritis back in the early 90's and the only thing that helped me was 800 milligrams of ibuprofen. But my Dr. said, "Let's make sure it's arthritis and not bursitis." So she ordered an MRI.

"The size of a newborn baby's head - What!"

"Yes, Ms. Ratliff. Your MRI shows that you have what looks like a dermoid tumor on your left ovary that measures the size of a newborn baby's head."

"So, what does that mean, and what's next?" Immediately my mind went to cancer.

"I cannot have cancer." That was all I could think about while she was talking.

"It doesn't necessarily mean cancer, so let's get another doctor to take a look before we send you to oncology. My cancer count was high, but she sad that didn't necessarily mean cancer. However, it did mean that something else was being sustained on my blood supply, and that is why I suffered from severe anemia.

My Dr. sent me across the hall to one of the other practicing gynecologists for an exam and another test. He stated, "We are not sure that it is cancer, but it has to come out asap." I told him that I was moving to North Carolina in a week and he said, "No matter where you move to – it has to come out – bottom line."

He was a very nice man. He even said that he would give me a tummy tuck in the process. I was all for it!

As soon as I left the Dr.'s office I called my mother. Her reaction was, "You have to come home for that surgery. I don't want you way out there with a surgery like that."

Well alright! Momma had spoken, so I made arrangements to have it done in Charlotte North Carolina.

The days were counting down. It was almost time to hit the road – heading back to North Carolina. Christy was sad, I was sad, everyone was sad – but I knew I had to go back.

March 30th was my last day at Gap. Tom left early that day because he didn't want to see me leave.

Everyone wished me well and sent me on my way.

Chapter 17

BINGO!

The surgery went very well, and as planned, momma took care of me during my healing process.

After I was released to return to my normal activities, I returned to church. My pastor put me back in position, and I resumed my responsibilities as intercessory prayer ministry leader. My outlook this time around was a whole lot better. I was now fortified to fight now.

Within four months of returning to church and prayer, I was promoted to being the personal assistant to the Bishop. This too was no surprise to me, as God had shown it to me in, yes, another night vision. This was one of the main reasons I was to return to Charlotte. I had an assignment to complete.

Things are going really well. I was traveling – again, and walking in what I believed to be my destiny. I was comfortable being right there, but God had other plans.

"Come on Erica, call my number!" G48! That was all I needed to win the jackpot that night, and it took every ounce of willpower in me to get it out.

"B-I-N-G-O!" It finally came out, and boy was I overjoyed. I'd hit the bonus for the night and oh how I needed it. That was a good night.

Back in 2008 my sister had invited me out to play bingo with her. I personally thought it was a waste of time and money at the time. You never know when and if you were going to win, so at first I didn't put a lot of heart into it. As a matter of fact, I complained of how boring it was, and how long it took ... until I started leaving with more than I went in with. Then it became interesting.

My sister was a huge risk taker. She would spend it all and say, "Oh well, you can't win 'em all." But I, on the other hand, was a totally different story. I would play, but I would not play my last. I remember her telling me,

"Tammie, scared money won't win." And I thought to myself, "Well honey, I guess I won't win then," because I was just never comfortable giving away my money. But the more I went – the more my philosophy changed. Yep! I was hooked on bingo.

There is this little place off of Eastway drive in Charlotte called Eastway bingo that she and I would frequent probably 2 to 3 times a week. Some nights it was good, and some nights it was bad. Playing 'games of chance' you just never know. We'd go in there and sit in our usual corner and laugh and just have a good time. We'd laugh until we both bout wet our pants, but it was so much fun.

Some of the regulars there just stared at us as if they were saying, "I wish they would stop all that laughing." Yeah, we cut up really bad. The one thing I can truly say about spending time with my sister was that she taught me how to laugh through some rough times. Growing up we never spent a lot of time getting to know each other. We just seemed to have different interest – even as young girls. But when she moved to Charlotte in 2003, I can honestly say I learned how to not take myself so serious.

I know you are wondering if I was playing bingo while I was actively attending church and working in ministry. Yes, I was. At first I felt really uneasy about going, but after a while it became a part of my normal routine. I didn't realize the impact it would have on my life later on.

"Tammie, let's go to the click."

"Huh? What in the world is the click click?"

"You know, the sweepstakes place." I'd heard about them on the news and I didn't want to get caught up into the gambling scene. Besides, I didn't think there was that much money to be won in those places anyway. So, I graciously declined …. at first.

My sister had somewhat graduated from the bingo hall, and now she was going to the internet café on a regular basis. For a long time, I would not go. But when she stopped going to bingo so did I. Her trips to the click click began to interest me. "Tammie, girl you ought to come – you'll love it," she would say. A part of me wanted to; while the other part of me did not want anyone to know that I was 'gambling', so to speak. I couldn't have anyone running back telling my pastor that I was sitting up in an internet café gambling. What would he think of me? What would those who looked up to me at church think? But somewhere between my "No" and her telling me about her "Winnings," I threw caution to the wind and went.

"Ok, this is not so bad. If anyone said something to me about seeing my car at one of these places I'll just tell them that I was using the internet." That was the liar's logic. But after a while I didn't even care. Now I was asking her (my sister) about going to the click click.

Again, we turned that into a regular outing. Some Saturdays we would spend all day and all of our money "at the click click." Bill money and all. To be honest, both of us had lost our grip on our responsibilities. As soon as money would hit our hand – we went to clicking. Here too, similar to bingo, sometimes it was good but the majority of the time it was bad. We spent hundreds at the time and didn't have gas to get to work the next day.

We'd sit there for hours and play. Our machines (money count) would build up, and instead of cashing out, something in our heads would say, "Play some more, the bonuses are coming." With those games, if you got all of your ducks or shamrocks, or whatever you were playing – in a row – you would win big. That is what kept so many of us there. Waiting for the big win. There were some people that got it – but I never did.

After getting evicted and losing everything, I had no desire to go near those places ever again. I would often say that there were demons in those places because you can go in with your mind set on playing twenty or forty dollars, but as soon as that is gone you are hitting the ATM machine for more. Unlike bingo, the cost involved at the internet café quadrupled. Due to the nature of the game – we would spend more money, quicker. I soon realized that I'd become addicted. I felt that if I could just go one more time, I would hit the big money. But that never happened. I think the most I'd ever won was somewhere close to five hundred dollars.

Shortly afterward my church life began to change. I was in transition again. My pastor and I decided that it was time to do something different, and so we parted ways. I knew God was moving me in a new direction, but it was one of the hardest separations I'd ever had to endure. Sometimes in separations, there's not a clear explanation other than it being time to move forward, and I left it at that.

I can't say that we had a major falling out because we didn't. I actually knew two months prior that I would be leaving the ministry because God had already revealed it to me. I just didn't know when. But the time had come, and it was time to go.

The Shift

Chapter 18

DIVINE ALIGNMENT

There comes a point in everyone's life when what use to work does not work anymore. Things become extremely difficult, and this could be a sure sign that your season may be changing.

In the church, the changing of seasons is a very prevalent topic. When God desires to move you from one place to another it can be very painful, but necessary. This is where I found myself in 2011.

What am I going to do now? I'd known this ministry for ten years. Where will I go? At the time of the separation, I had no idea of where my "next" would be. I was so accustomed to hearing the voice of that experience – what could measure up to this?

Being in the church and in ministry as I was, I felt naked without the affiliation. But after the separation, God began to speak to me about 'me'. He said, "I am taking you somewhere, but you can't go like you are."

"Huh? What's wrong with me?"
I thought I was alright. After all, I was over the prayer ministry at church, traveling with my pastor and I'd become a source of wisdom to a handful of people.

"Hey, I'm doing quite alright."

Boy was I full of myself. When God tells you that something is wrong with you and you question Him – something is terribly wrong – with you.

I'm reading my bible and the Lord leads me to Joshua 5. It's the story of Joshua and the children of Israel crossing over the Jordan into Gilgal. They were not quite to the promise land, but they were closer than they'd ever been. As they pitched their tent in Gilgal God instructed Joshua to circumcise them again. There was a new generation among them that had not experienced the circumcision, and it was Joshua's responsibility to get it done. As I continued to read the chapter the Lord revealed to me something in vs.8 that would give me clarity about the process I was about to go through.

"And it came to pass, when they had done circumcising all the people, that they abode in their places in the camp, till they were whole." Joshua 5:8

"Until they were whole." I was not whole. God had brought me to this place to bring me to a place of wholeness. Within the next year, I would come to know this place as "The Middle." "You are not where you were, but you are not quite where you are going

– but you are, however, somewhere in the middle."

The Middle is that place where God cleanses your heart. He cuts away the unnecessary things in order to get the best use of your life. This is called circumcision. Some call it the "wilderness," while others call it "going through." However you choose to reference it – it still equals out to the same experience of preparation for where you are headed.

One of the first things the Lord showed me was that when you are in this place you have to release your old experiences. The bible said in Joshua 5:12, "And the manna ceased .... But they did eat of the fruit of Canaan that year."

It was time for me to let go of the old and embrace the new. The old what? The new what? I really wasn't sure what that was because I was just fine like I was – so I thought.

December has come, and I am invited to a New Year's service. The preacher is going in, and he turns and looks at me, and tells his assistant to come get me. I stand at the altar for a while before he says anything to me. Then finally he comes over and begins to pour life into my dry bones.

When you are in a place of uncertainty it can leave you depleted. I was no longer a part of anything and

I had no clue as to what was coming. So as he spoke he brought hope back to me. He told me that I'd been hiding long enough, and it was time for me to walk in the call of God upon my life. He exposed the real reason that I had not pursued purpose – fear. But he reassured me that God was about to do something major in my life.

We made a connection, and in the months following I was ordained an Elder in the Lord's Church. But let's not forget, I was still on a journey to wholeness, so being ordained was not the ultimate crossover for me. There was yet a greater work that needed to take place. One that only God could do.

It's New Year's Eve and the prophetic announcement has been made. "2012 is the year of divine alignment, and God is shifting some things into order in your life.

"Praise the Lord! It's finally coming together. God is going to do this great thing in my life this year, and I'm ready." I was beyond excited. I just knew I would be in a new place, doing new things, among new people. By this time, I'd made a decision to move to Maryland where my new leader was, so I gave up my house and moved in with my sister with the hopes of relocating and walking in my "Next.

Chapter 19

THE BIG REVEAL

Moving in with my sister and her children was definitely a setup. The truth was about to come out.

"You wanna do coffee?"

"Yes, ma'am."

I was so excited to share this space with her – but not necessarily everything that came along with her. A house full of teenagers who were coming into their own coupled with a religious mindset was not a good mix, but I thought my presence would change all of that.

Our coffee times were really special. Every morning we would either have coffee at home, or we would stop somewhere on the way to our jobs. In my mind, I would add so much to her life – but in time, she would teach me one of the greatest lessons of my life.

"Tammie, I found this little spot down on South Blvd. you might like." Yep, she was clickin' again, and it wouldn't be long before I followed. It was something about us doing it together that made it intriguing. Not only was it intriguing, but it was addictive. I knew I'd vowed to never go into those place ever again – but I couldn't help it.

"Let's go!" I was gung-ho.

Again, we found ourselves sitting there for hours on end trying to win big, leaving broke busted and disgusted. But this time our clicking stint didn't last that long. I was getting serious about moving and making preparation for that, and she had a new boyfriend.

I was not happy because I felt like she should be pursuing the things of God instead of a man. So, the mean girl began to come out. I had a prescribed way of how people should live, especially women, and that did not include sleeping around. She was not doing that, but I felt that she should get into the church and allow God to bring someone into her life.

I'd been celibate for some time, and I felt that everyone who was not married should live like me. The thing that I didn't realize was that not everyone was where I was as it relates to relationships. You see, I'd come to a place in my life where I refused to be in another loveless, sex-filled relationship. I'd had my share of encounters like that, and at this point in my life I needed more from a relationship.

She was spending a lot of time with her new beau and I was spending my time preparing to leave. I'd gotten a new truck and left my job at Wells Fargo, anticipating God opening a door for me to leave. When it didn't open, I took a leap of what I thought was faith and pushed it open.

"I'm finally here!" I knew this would be the start of something great. Shortly after arriving I landed a part-time job that was looking very promising, however, things changed with my living arrangements there, and I had to come back to North Carolina. I didn't have enough money to rent a room or anything so back to Charlotte I went.

Whew! Finally made it back. That visit to Maryland was interesting to say the least. The job was simple enough, though. I mean how many ways can you transfer a call. But anyway, "Charlotte, how you doin'?"

Now, I just have to figure out my next move. Shall I stay or shall I return? That was the question of the day on May 28, 2012.

I knew the Lord was leading me to Maryland, but it seemed that although the door opened – it quickly closed. Two weeks in and I am back in Charlotte. Talking about confused. Lord have mercy. "I guess I'll just hang out in Charlotte until something more definite happens up that way." That was my logic.

"Hey, good people!" Walking back into my sister's home was not a good feeling to me. I felt like I was going back into the den of the disapproved. But I had to put on the good ole Christian greeting. Knowing in my heart I did not want to be there around "those people."

"So, what's up?" Just trying to make small talk while I packed my son up to go live with his dad. Nobody really responded because we all knew that I was a ticking time bomb waiting to blow-up, and at that point it really didn't matter who responded to whom. I just wanted to get Mate and leave.

On my way back to Charlotte from dropping Mate off I thought about all of the things that I had to endure in that house with them. "Lord, why do I have to go back there." I mean, I thought I would be settled in Maryland by now and wouldn't have to deal with them anymore. I was so self-righteous. "Oh well, I guess God has a greater plan than me, so I will just make the best of it."

When I got back to the house I got this sudden taste for some spaghetti. You know that good ole cheesy baked spaghetti. "Yummy," I thought as I was sitting in my truck dreading to go into that house. Something felt real funny, but I didn't feed too much into it, so I pulled right back out of the driveway heading to the grocery store.

Going to Aldi I recognized a wrecker a few cars behind me but I was only a car payment behind so it didn't strike me as too unusual. I pull into Aldi – and the wrecker does too. But it still didn't register that they were following me. I parked – they parked. The driver goes in and then I go in. "Ok, good! They are not here for me."

As I am standing in line I notice that the wrecker has pulled around to my truck and now has my truck hooked up to his hitch. "Oh My God No!" I jetted out of the store and pled with them to not take it, but to no avail. With a wimpy apology from them, they still refused to release it. But they did offer to take me home.

Once I arrived home (to my sister's house) there they were standing outside. "What are ya'll looking at?" I thought. I was furious, embarrassed and all of the above ... ten times over.

Why did this have to happen while they looked on? The driver and his passenger helped me to unload all of my belongings from the vehicle before they left. "Jesus! What is going on?" I was infuriated, as well as, in utter shock. No notice or anything. No opportunity to work it out, nothing.

"Lord!" I was distraught. I'd lost more than my

share of vehicles through repossession, but not like this. Not at a time like this. I'd taken what I thought to be the right steps toward "fulfilling my destiny" by agreeing to move to Maryland, and now God has allowed my car to be taken? How cruel is that! I was really disappointed. I didn't think I would recover. I'd lost so much over the course of my life, and I just couldn't take another loss. Besides, according to the Word of the Lord for the year 2012 – it was the year of Divine Alignment. So how could this be remotely close to a 'divine alignment' of any kind?

I'd just gotten the truck in February, and here it was only May and it's gone. I felt as low as you can get. This is not supposed to be happening to me – NOT AGAIN! How am I supposed to get to Maryland now? How was I supposed to fulfill my ministry assignment now? "Lord, just take me."

Those were the words I mustered up after laying in the bed for almost two weeks, depressed. "Lord, I will never get it right so just take me in my sleep." I never had a desire to commit suicide myself, but I did, however, want God to take me. I just felt like this walk with God was too hard, and that I would never get it right. I was just plain ole tired of struggling with it.

The humiliation I had to endure – watching "them"

live like what I described as 'heathens', yet still appear to be functioning ok. Here I am, the prayer warrior, the one who'd led the corporate prayer at my previous church, traveling with the Bishop and being ordained an Elder a few months prior. Why Was This Happening To ME? I'm the good one!

I found myself experiencing a plethora of emotions – all related to my previous works in the church. I thought God should have shown me a little more mercy since I had done so much (in my own mind) to build His Kingdom. I mean really God; you couldn't have given me at least some type notice?

"Yeah, just take me. I can't do this anymore." I felt like I was taking one step forward and a hundred steps backward. This had been the story of my life and I was tired! I figured that if He took me, at least I would make it to heaven before I could make any more bad decisions here on earth. I thought for sure I was ready to go.

One afternoon, after about a full 2 weeks of sulking, I heard the Holy Spirit say, "Get up." I obeyed, not because I wanted to but because His voice was so loud and clear. He began to instruct me to 'forgive myself.' Me, with my self-righteous self, thought, "What for? I've already forgiven myself." He said, "No you haven't," and proceeded to show me my life right before my eyes. The many times I was dishonest and had not operated in integrity. The many times, when I was younger, that I'd slept with other women's husbands – thinking it was ok. He showed me the depth of guilt and shame I'd carried for getting pregnant at 17 and lying to my parents about it – causing them great shame. The many times I'd taken that which did not belong to me – causing other people great despair. No, I hadn't forgiven myself for all of that.

I'd gotten saved and carried all of that guilt and negative self-talk with me. I read the bible, but because I was so burdened with guilt, unworthiness, shame and condemnation I could not seem to embrace the love of God for a person such as myself.

I felt that I was the worse of the worse, but through my works at the church I thought I could please God. I felt that I could prove to God that I was a pretty decent person, even though I didn't even believe it. Little did I know that God had already forgiven me – it was Tammie who was holding herself hostage.

It was Tammie who was feeding her mind the chatter of unworthiness. It was Tammie who had not received God's forgiveness.

I realized through this ordeal that I never really embraced God's love because I never understood what love really was. I'd grown up in an organization that painted a picture of God as being "the punisher." If you did bad, He was waiting to get you.

I could quote the scriptures to those who were down and out, but I could not apply them to my own life. During this time, I had to come face to face with the reality of my own condescending thinking. I just didn't feel worthy, so I couldn't accept God's love and forgiveness.

As I continued this process with the Holy Spirit, speaking out loud – "Tammie I forgive you" – I literally felt the heaviness fall off of me. The weight of disappointment and the coat of despair were finally being removed from my shoulders and my mind. It really felt like chains were falling off of me. I felt a shimmer of hope for my life. I felt like I could get up and go on.

Right in my moments of revelation I began to study the life of Job. What a revealing. I never equated my life to one who was prideful. Never in a million years did I see me as high-minded. I mean, I was told that I had a sweet spirit and all. I could prophesy. I could minister encouragement to people through my writings. So, me, being prideful? Nope, not me. But in actuality it was ME.

I was a woman who had low self-esteem, an

unworthy mentality, a guilty conscience and feelings of hopelessness all my life. A woman who was always recognized for her gifts and abilities, but not for the precious creation she was. A woman who felt that as long as she could make you happy, she was acceptable.

I didn't know my worth. I didn't know who I was. My identity was wrapped up in the gift(s) and not in the free gift of being loved by an Almighty Merciful God. A God who looked beyond my faults and saw my need for help.

I didn't realize that the mere fact that He allowed me to be born was an indication that there was a purpose for my life. I came to understand that He uniquely made me and gave me a portion of Himself (the Holy Spirit), making me all the more valuable.

Me? The deceiver! Me? The liar! Me? The adulterer! Me? The one who had no real concern for others – only what I could get from them. Me? God loved Me? That was so humbling. I finally understood the cause of Christ. A man who died for people who were just like Me. A man who laid the groundwork for those who felt helpless and hopeless that we might have a relationship with the Father. God really does love us!

Through the legend of the Acura MDX truck – the

conversion experience was beginning. A change of heart was happening, and a greater understanding was materializing. God was simply allowing me to see what I thought I already knew.

Chapter 20

THE THINGS YOU CAN SEE IN THE DARK

Whoa! Job was a character. During my depressive downtime, I began to read the book of Job, and boy oh boy did God speak to me about me through that book. It was if I'd relived a degree of Job's experience. Beyond the losses, I'd experienced the agony of wanting to die. I felt as if I'd done enough church work to ensure my positioning in heaven and I was ready to go. Man-o-man was my perspective wrong, but God still wasn't done with me yet.

"Lord have mercy they are in and out, smoking weed and drinking, and Lord knows what else. How am I still stuck in this place?" At the time, all I could see was "they." What "they" were doing. In my own self-righteous mind, God was highly upset with them and so was I. I felt like they could care less about God, and it made me very angry. So I took it upon myself to behave in a way that was sure to let them know that God was not pleased with them. How wrong was that?

It was now June, and it was my responsibility to pay the light bill. "Tuh, I hope I do pay this bill while they are hanging out being disrespectful." At the core of my mentality was punishment, and making them pay. In my twisted mind, I felt that they deserved to be in the dark because they were not living right. The sad part about it was that I felt like I was right. I didn't realize that I was actually expressing my own disdain for myself and the cloud of unforgiveness that I lived under in my own life. It's called projection. The images and feelings I had of myself – I projected onto to them.

Click! Everything went off. "What the world!" I jumped to my feet to see what happened. Oh God! It was Duke Energy. They'd cut the lights off. Although I was shocked, I realized that there was nothing I could do. My unemployment had run out and I had nothing. It was not my sister's pay week so I knew she didn't have anything, so I did an about-face and retreated back upstairs, sinking deeper into the bed of my despair.

The reality of my mentality had manifested. My lack of concern had shown up in a way that was undeniable. We were now "in the dark," in mid-June - in 95 plus degree weather.

"What have I done?" Now, everyone was suffering because of me. All because of my self-righteous attitude. All because I thought that they didn't deserve God's goodness. All because I simply didn't care.

I remember thinking, "How could you be so mean Tammie?" But almost instantly the brother to self-righteousness, which is justification, spoke up, "They deserve it." I thought that maybe now they would acknowledge God and stop sinning." But the real truth was – God was allowing me to see my own treacherous heart. He used that experience to show me how I really felt underneath all of the sugar coated bible talk. He exposed the woman that had been running the show to the woman that I was becoming. He exposed the one who thought she could hide behind the church. The one whose mode of operation was guilt, shame, and most of all fear.

Still, I wavered back and forth in my mind, "You're wrong for this."

"No, it's not your responsibility to take care of people who could care less about their lives."

My mind was taking me back and forth, forth and back. Never once did I embrace the fact that I should've been a part of the solution, and not the problem. Oh yeah, I knew right from wrong in my head, but my heart was not able to conceptualize this concept. I was stuck in my own perception of the way things ought to be.

Everyone in the house watched me as if I was some kind of monster. They didn't know from day to day how I would act or react towards them. I could tell in their eyes that they were confused when it came to me. There were times when I prayed with them and it was powerful, but then there were times when I'd go on a rant about their lifestyles – condemning them and putting them down. Religion had done a fine job of redefining Christianity for me.

"It were better for him that a millstone were hanged about his neck, and he cast into the sea, than that he should offend one of these little ones."
Luke 17:2

But my turning point came one day when I looked into my oldest niece's eyes and heard the Lord say, "There are some people that it's best that you just leave them alone. Don't say anything to them if it means you will offend them." My heart sunk deep into my lower abdomen, later finding its way to my knees. That's when I realized the source of my trouble with God.

He said to me, "If you can't help them – don't hurt them." And that's what I'd been doing all along. I had no concept of the genuine heart of God towards people because I was bound by my own religious insight. I was operating by a law that said if you're not going to church and living "right" – you don't deserve a good life.

I felt like if you weren't performing all of the religious rituals then you were not worthy of God's goodness. Yes, I knew that He loved us, but by my definition it was conditional.

How could goodness (God) look on people who were doing everything contrary to what He stood for – and bless them? How? In my calculations, it just was not possible ... until I read the following scripture in Hebrews 8:10, 12, and it reads:

"For this is the covenant that I will make with the house of Israel. After those days, saith the Lord, I will put my laws in their mind, and write them in their hearts. And I will be to them a God, and they will be to me a people." 12 "For I will be merciful to their unrighteousness, and their sins and their iniquities will I remember no more."

Huh? I'd never comprehended it in this way. As a matter of fact – I'd never read this scripture. I was truly undergoing a conversion experience. A lot of what I'd been taught was not according to the teachings of Christ.

My eyes were beginning to open, and the scales

that had been placed there by the doctrines of men were falling away. I was finally realizing what the gospel (The Good News) of Jesus Christ was really about. The perfect law of love.

Now I get it! Now – it is all coming together for me. It was as if I was finally accepting the fact that God knew everything about us – the good, the bad and the ugly, but still chose to love us anyway. I'd finally come to truly understand that it was because of our messed-up state that Jesus needed to die for us.

There had to be a perfect, unblemished sacrifice made for our return. And now He sees us the way He'd intended for us to be from the beginning of time.

The final stages of the softening were taking root.

Chapter 21

WITH CHANGE COMES CHALLENGE

"Finally, it's December 2012, and I am leaving North Carolina. I am finally on my way to Maryland for sure this time.

I'd just birthed two books within a matter of months, and the way has been made for me to move to Maryland. The books were not in my plan, but the nuggets I received during my time with my sister I had to savor. I'd learned so much during my season of conversion and I knew that at some point in the future someone else would benefit from what I'd gained.

I am blasting my resume everywhere. No one is calling, then finally near the end of January Finiti Title calls. I'm granted an interview and within 30 minutes of leaving the interview I get the offer call.

"Can you start on Monday?"

"Yes, I can." Yes! God was already moving. Finiti was a title company that handled refinanced mortgage loans, and with a background in real estate I knew I would love it.

I started off in title commitment and quickly

moved to escalations. This was a position that made sure all the loan components were in before closing. It was a great position. My manager, Kay, and I hit it off immediately. She recognized that there was more in me than met the eye, and she purposed in her heart to push me to be the very best I could be – on the job and off.

You see, Kay was a minister as well. She was well versed in the word, and could articulate it with great skill. Our friendship grew quickly, and because of her I got an invite to share my book at her church.

> God moves in His timing. "For my thoughts are not your thoughts, neither are your ways my ways." declares the Lord.
>
> Isaiah 55:8

It was a different experience because it was a universal church. I'd never considered ministering to a universal congregation, but the "Matters of the Heart" message has no boundaries.

It was phenomenal! Her pastor bought twenty books and gave them to some of the women who'd come to the conference from the women's shelter. He then allowed me to do a book signing. I ended up selling everything I had that day. Wow! God showed up in an amazing way that day. If God had not done a work in my heart, I would have missed that opportunity.

Shortly afterwards I began to experience an uneasiness in my environment. I felt that religious spirit creeping around. Soon the great confrontation came. "Nobody will ever read anything you've written, nor will they listen to anything you say when they see that mug shot of you online."

"Really! Well, you are referring to "church folk," and I could care less about what they think about me because I am not called to them." I was livid that someone could attempt to discredit me because of what they knew about my past, especially someone of the faith.

It was that conversation right there that solidified my stance to love the unlovable, and minister to the broken. I was more determined than ever not to be like them. They were the epitome of what God had delivered me from, and I'd made a resolve never to return to my own vomit (old way of thinking).

God had freed me from that critical, judgmental, unworthy mentality and the enemy was using someone close to me to pull me back into his clutches. I knew, just through that conversation that my tenure was up.

When God brings about a true change in your heart you will be confronted and challenged. Confronted with the suggestive undertone of, "You haven't really changed," and challenged in the area of your deliverance. Will you fight fire with fire, or will you fight with the Words of our Lord, "It is written." I could have easily fired back with what I knew of them, but that is not how you win spiritual battles. My desire was to maintain my freedom in Christ – even if it meant walking away.

The opportunity came for me to do just that, and I was glad. I'd accomplished my assignment there and it was again, time to go, and I have never looked back.

I'd gotten me another car and God opened the door for me to transition back to North Carolina.

I know you are probably thinking that it did not take all of that for me to finally experience my freedom, but yes it did. I had to be tested before I could be trusted. God wanted me to see the change that He'd done in me. A change that was genuine, and liberating.

When you can go back into the environment that God brought you out of and not partake of their fruit – you are free, and free indeed. When God delivers you from a thing, it becomes a stench in your nostrils. God delivered me from liquor, and to this day I cannot stand the way it smells.

It reminds me of what Jesus said in John 14:30, "I will not say much more to you, for the prince of this world is coming, and he has nothing in me." One translation says, " ... He has no power over me." (ISV)

Real deliverance is liberating. The thing that held you no longer has control over you. It is an inner working like none other.

Sometimes God has to take us through many things before we can see ourselves. However, in doing so, and as we acknowledge our helpless state, He can turn us into another man/woman. The person He originally created us to be.

As Jacob was with the angel of the Lord in Genesis 32:26, we must also be. We must make the resolve to hold onto God until he blesses us and changes our name. And in changing our name – He changes our nature.

Chapter 22

MATTERS OF THE HEART

Religion has really hurt a lot of people. Many think, as did I, from a pharisaic mindset – "The more you do, the better you are." They have an elitist mentality. But this way of thinking leads us to a place of pride, and the bible says in James 4:6, "God opposes the proud but shows favor to the humble."

What does it mean to be humble? Glad you asked. According to Dictionary.com, humility is defined as, "modest opinion or estimate of one's own importance, rank, etc." One of its synonyms is a word that many of us cringe at the very annunciation of it – submission. However, when this word is used as it relates to the life of a believer, its highest use is referring to our surrendering to the authority of God, through both the written and the Rhema Word.

For many years humility had an appearance. I could look the part, but submission was far from my heart, so there had to come a fall in my life. God had been trying to get my attention for many years, but I was just too full of myself to listen. The heart is a deceiver, who can truly know it?

After months of writing, I was finally able to say, as Job in Job 42:5, "I have heard of thee by the hearing of the ear: but now mine eyes seeth thee."

My problem was not church attendance. I was faithful in that area, as you have read. However, my problem was a warped perception of myself, others, and God. And through a lifelong journey He's made the correction. I'd been saved for twenty-two years, but was converted in 2012. Peter walked with the Christ for three years and was still shaky in his conviction. He too needed to be converted before he could fulfill his destiny.

> "The wind blows where it wishes, and you hear its sound, but you do not know where it comes from or where it goes. So it is with everyone who is born of the Spirit."
> John 3:8

"But I have prayed for you, Simon, that your faith fail not; and when you are converted, strengthen the brethren." Luke 22:32

This is one of my staple scriptures today. We cannot fulfill our destiny in God unless we have experienced a change of heart. Peter had a change of heart. He'd made up in his mind that he was going to do it God's way, no matter what. And when you get this mindset then you can help someone else – and nothing can by any means stop you!

Another one of my favorite passages of scripture, up to this point, had been Psalm 51:10, *"Create in me a clean heart, O' God, and renew a right spirit within me."* But, He didn't just create in me a clean heart and give me a renewed spirit, He gave me a new heart. A heart of flesh in exchange for my stony heart.

He gave me a heart that is sympathetic to the needs of others. He gave me a heart that is capable of sincere, unconditional love. He gave me a heart that could let go and forgive. Not just others, but myself in particular.

It has been through my journey that God has brought me to a place of wholeness in Him. It has been through my many internal struggles that the spirit of God has exposed the hidden places in my soul and brought forth liberty.

When we know better, we must do better. The process of beComing who God has predetermined us to be is continuously unfolding in each one of us. However, we must choose to accept and participate in that process. You will not know when the change occurs, but you will be well aware of the fact that a change has definitely taken place. This is the true born-again experience.

EPILOGUE

Coming Clean is a message I wrote a few years ago. I was in a major place of reflection, and knew that if I did not acknowledge my then state, I could not move forward in wholeness.

Today, as I am finishing up this book, I must say that it has really caused me to reflect on my life in a real way. Too many of us want to experience that abundant life that we read about in the Word of God, but we are stuck. We're stuck in emotional cycles, mental cycles, and even spiritual cycles.

Day in, and day out, we feed our minds negative self-talk that only cultivate defeat. We all have been hurt. We all have hurt people. However, it is time for you to forgive yourself, and move forward.

This has been the story of my life. I could only get so far in life before the chatter started. "You don't deserve this. Look at the things you've done." "Who do you think you are?" And on, and on it went. But in 2012, I realized that was not the voice of God – it was my own guilty, shameful, unworthy attitude towards myself speaking.

My own negative chatter that stemmed from my own negative self-image. But today, I AM FREE! And it is time for you to get free too. I don't dot every I, nor do I cross every T. But I am a much better person today than I was yesterday.

So I say to you, "You are not your past experiences." As shaming as they may be, they can no longer hold you hostage. Everyone has a past, so don't you dare live in condemnation. And do not allow the rudiments of religion to dictate God's love and favor towards you. You have not done too much, and you have not gone too far outside of the reach of God. Man may cast you off, but God will *never leave nor forsake you*. This is something that after being saved twenty-two years – I had to learn to embrace. God IS for you!

Our Father is so good to us, and in turn we must reflect His goodness in the earth. I stand whole-heartedly on this saying, "If you can't help someone – don't hurt them." My life today is so much richer now that I have learned that lesson. I now value family and friends. I now see them through the eyes of God, instead of through the eyes of criticism and judgmentalism.

To that end, don't despise your trials, no matter how many times you have come to this place. Just know that God is trying to purify your heart for the next leg of life's journey. Be encouraged, and know this: "You are not where you were, but you are not quite where you were, but you are however, "Somewhere in the Middle." And you cannot move forward in wholeness until you: acknowledge your stuff, come clean, and walk in forgiveness - starting with the forgiveness of yourself.

Look Up – He Still Has A Plan For Your Life!

ABOUT THE AUTHOR

Tammie Michelle Ratliff was raised in Detroit, Michigan. The third child of seven children.

Not having the experience of growing up in the church, Tammie would soon realize, through circumstances, her need for God. After receiving a DWI in 1989, she would no longer continue on her destructive course of alcoholism. In 1990 she accepted Christ as her Lord and Savior while sitting in her car. Determined not to spend eternity in hell, she pursued hard after God.

In 1995 She joined Kings Gate Church (formerly known as Sierra Christian Center), under the leadership of Pastor Eddie & Jeannie Mclean. It was here that she would learn the fundamental truths of God's Word. It was also at Sierra that she would receive several certificates of study through the school of ministry. In 2000, she received the call of God to teach His Word, and immediately following – moved to Charlotte North Carolina.

In 2001 she joined Temple Church International, under the leadership of Bishop Kevin Long. Here she served as intercessory prayer leader for a total of four years. After which, she served as the assistant to the Bishop for three years.

Pursuant further studies, in 2012 Tammie was ordained an Elder in The Word Harvest International Fellowship of Churches, under the leadership of James Lemuel Spence, where she presently serves. Tammie is also the founder of Tammie Ratliff Ministries, under which she holds her semi-annual "Matters of the Heart" gathering.

She is the author of four books to date; The A.M. Deposit, a 40 Day Compilation of Writings from The Cave of Adullam; The Shower Talks series, (Vol. I and II) – Devotional books of "Selah Moments from My Secret Place with the Father," and her latest release, "Coming Clean – Journey to Wholeness. She also shares inspirational moments on Facebook through The A.M. Deposit Facebook page.

Tammie has two boys and currently resides in Charlotte North Carolina.

Other Titles by Tammie Ratliff

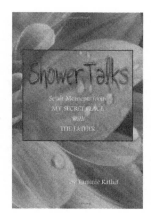

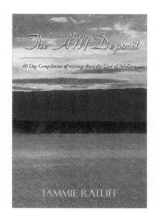

Available on Amazon.com
Also Available @Tammieratliff.com